Things people may have said

"Delightfully flawed"
"Preposterously compelling"
"Brutally irresistible"
"Unequivocally necessary"
"Hilariously incisive"
"Masochistically rapturous"
"At bloody last"

UN-F★CKING WORK

WORK

How to fix it for good

UN-F★CKING WORK

WORK

How to fix it for good

Neil Usher

Winchester, UK
Washington, USA

JOHN HUNT PUBLISHING

First published by Zero Books, 2022
Zero Books is an imprint of John Hunt Publishing Ltd., No. 3 East St., Alresford,
Hampshire SO24 9EE, UK
office@jhpbooks.com
www.johnhuntpublishing.com
www.zero-books.net

For distributor details and how to order please visit the 'Ordering' section on our website.

Text copyright: Neil Usher 2021

ISBN: 978 1 78535 951 4
978 1 78535 952 1 (ebook)
Library of Congress Control Number: 2021942800

A CIP catalogue record for this book is available from the British Library.

Design: Stuart Davies

UK: Printed and bound by CPI Group (UK) Ltd, Croydon, CR0 4YY
Printed in North America by CPI GPS partners

We operate a distinctive and ethical publishing philosophy in
all areas of our business, from our global network of authors to
production and worldwide distribution.

Contents

A quiet word   1

Chapter 1: "We are where we are"   3
Chapter 2: "Work is something we do, not a place we go"   11
Chapter 3: "Hard work never hurt anyone"   24
Chapter 4: "It's not a blame culture"   40
Chapter 5: "We trust our people"   55
Chapter 6: "We're an equal opportunities employer"   70
Chapter 7: "Culture eats strategy for breakfast"   85
Chapter 8: "If it ain't broke, don't fix it"   99
Chapter 9: "Teamwork makes the dream work"   112
Chapter 10: "If we can't measure it, we can't manage it"   125
Chapter 11: "People are our greatest asset"   137
Chapter 12: "We're like a big start-up"   151
Chapter 13: "This is a great place to work"   160
Chapter 14: We are where we're going   173

Petit fours   180
Endnotes   185
Biographies   196

This book is dedicated to all those who didn't get in the helicopter, circle back, run it up a flagpole, take it offline, shift a paradigm, touch base, punch a puppy, spin plates, break eggs, boil the ocean, put a pin in it, roll a turd in glitter or think outside the damn box.

* * *

And all those who did.

Acknowledgments

Very special thanks for encouragement, advice and honesty to Susan Furber, Adrienne Skelton, Amelia Saberwal, Gareth Jones, Jessica Bailey, Anne Marie Rattray, Stephen Logan, Catalina Contoloru, Mark Eltringham and Gem Dale.

A Quiet Word

This isn't a "business" book. It's probably in the business book section of the website or shop because some works have no natural home.

It doesn't belong because business books perpetuate the world of work to which we've become accustomed. They offer momentary hope and inspiration through theories and models, rinsed and repeated, methods born of reading too many other business books. "Don't do that, do *this!*" But they don't challenge the fundamental precepts that underly their pitch. They're built on sand.

Like this.

We've been contacted about an opportunity. Our online profile is bang up to date, rich in detail. It effortlessly links to our website and blog. We're then asked for our CV. Which contains all the same information as that online. What do we do? We send our CV. Because if we don't, we won't be considered, while others who send their CV will. Although it's ridiculous, we'll never change things alone. That's how it works. We comply. Our present and future, our livelihood, our career; they're all at stake.

That's how it operates. At every level, at every scale.

So you picked up this book.

It's not going to hold your hand and tell you everything's going to be okay.

It's not going to tell you that the author and collaborators found the secret and solved everything and therefore so can you.

It's not going to offer top tips on achieving inner equilibrium – take a lunch break, you'll feel better in the afternoon.

But that's not *why* you picked up this book.

Here's what awaits.

Twelve common statements are presented that characterize and reinforce the world of work we've come to know. That is, all work. Not just that which occurs in the easiest fat-arsed squatting duck of targets, the hapless office, with its rituals and theatrics. Because whatever we do, we hear them all the time. We probably repeat them, sometimes even without embarrassment. Each statement is dismantled to reveal its inherent absurdities.

Suggestions are made as to how we can begin to rebuild from the rubble of each – three for each statement, all summarized at the end. But it's not a 36-point plan to cut out and keep, to pin on the wall. While not a business book, this isn't a repair manual either. How we rebuild work is fundamentally up to us. Personally and together. Driven by our energy and desire. To create the world of work we want. It'll never be a finished product. We don't get to rest.

After reading, we may initially do nothing, it's a natural response. But it'll have taken root. We'll be aware of each phrase when uttered, or worse, when we use one. Like a sleeper cell being activated. And then we'll want to do something about it. No, we'll *have* to do something about it.

As of today – this very moment – there's no going back.

Chapter 1

"We are where we are"

Work is fucked. Universally. The overriding illusion is that it's not. That there's enough potential for resilience to counter stress, determination to carve through anxiety, and discoverable resource to provide the tools and approaches to navigate the present and cling on to just enough optimism for the future.

Yet to compound the issue, work is often not entirely fucked. There are shards of light, successes, achievements, inspiring interactions, signs that what may have been weighing heavily on us is lifting. We scroll through our labors, the small, unpredictable rewards feeding our indomitable spirit. We emerge from setbacks to push on again.

We instinctively flag our disquiet early. When we feel crushed, what we mean is we're starting to feel crushed. When we say we can't take anymore we're saying we can take some more but probably not too much so please be careful with us. We don't actually know where the edge of the abyss lies, as it's shrouded in the fog that's led us there. We don't stare into the void because we're not sure we've reached it or what defines it and even less sure what it looks like. We assume it's down, that if we're to be consumed by it then it's by falling, that somehow, we'll have reached an edge – but it may not be. It may just be the path we're on. We may never get a chance to see it before we're consumed by it because we just don't know.

When confronted with what to do about it we're simply Stockholm-syndrome contentedly stuck. We say we want more benevolent employers, more flexibility, more concern for our wellbeing. Yet when we're given space, freedom and latitude, we manage to contrive to waste it or abuse it. This isn't something being done to us. We're helping out, too. Complicit.

The sedative is validation. We're okay with being stuck in a shit world of work we don't want to disrupt in case it reveals that we're not as hard-working, accountable, creative, diligent, applied, considered, kind or inventive as we might say "they" stop us from being. The need for validation makes us nauseous. Ill, even. Conveniently excusing ourselves with "the company won't allow me to..." means we don't have to reveal whether we really are bereft of those attributes. We just keep on seeking validation. Am I good enough?

As humans we soldier on. It was Kurt Vonnegut's character Kilgour Trout in *Breakfast of Champions* who'd been given "a life not worth living, but...an iron will to live."[1] Not just Kilgour, of course. The hope we carry is immense, and the spirit formidable. We trade fucked work for other fucked work. We wonder why it feels different but the same. We become progressively less aware of difference. The value we hold for one another elevates us above much of this habituation, a "shared higher thirst for an ideal above [us]," as Nietzsche rather beautifully described friendship. We crave it and it pays out. In this regard we often underestimate the power of the friendship, care and support we freely give. Together, we un-fuck just enough of work to be back tomorrow. And the day after.

Outside of that cordiality, sometimes within, somehow in our working lives it all comes back to other people. What they say and do, and what they don't say and don't do. As those versed in technical language would say "acts and omissions." Most of the time it's benign. But when it isn't, the effect is entirely disproportionate. Very often they're unintentional, or at least when intentional their consequences are often not anticipated. That's because the effects are cumulative. We consider the acts or omissions for which we're responsible in isolation. What seems minor or isolated to us rarely is to the recipient.

Except, of course, when it's final. Termination. The end of work. A word almost deliberately sequestrated for its ugliness. It runs parallel to the end of life itself. Where the act is intentional and its consequences known, despite the bearer of the news being unable to offer any solace or solution. A decision has been made. It is what it is, we are where we are. There's no understanding of it beyond rejection. On occasion, it may transpire to be a blessed relief, that a relationship has been finally called out as offensive and needs to end. The calling out is always far more difficult than the end itself.

That's because very often the experience is one of an abusive relationship. Rarely physical – though that isn't out of the question, by any means, even as a threat – more likely emotional and psychological. Characterized by irrationality, unpredictability, cruelty, jealously, unfairness and spite. It's often propagated by one person, someone who circumstance appears powerless to remove. On occasions it feels institutional, the way of things, leaving nowhere to turn. Everyone we look to wears an identical mask. Such situations also have a way of turning the victim into the cause, of folding both the sense and reality of justice back on itself.

At the "exit interview," a brief and final pause where honesty may at last find a glimmer of light, we wonder whether after all we've been through it's actually worth it. We've rehearsed the blistering tirade to ourselves so many times. At 3am we're incredible, destructively withering, irresistible. But when it arrives, we're not. We teeter on the pathetic. We offer that it's been a learning experience, the now familiar disguise for sheer, unabated and relentless torture. From the seduction of the entirely misleading advertisement to the handing back of the laptop, password on a sticky note. That is, we take no joy from it, just a warning that we'll try not to get ourselves into anything like this again.

Meanwhile, back in the cave, while relationships interplay, we're expected to get things done. We have a value statement to make each year to justify our continued inclusion, assessed by others with occasional reference to data, metrics, something tangible. We have sold, saved, processed, invented, connected or rejected enough. We missed the arbitrary "stretch" target, intentionally placed just out of reach. The agent of motivation worked. It's always annual and always individual. Even though dates are bookends of convenience only and we daily work with, and are reliant upon, others. As they are on us. Luck, an everyday feature of the interconnectedness of our lives, has no identity or visibility at an annual appraisal. Shit happens but someone's always accountable. It's usually the person closest to the actual shit happening.

Which is why we constantly strive to be furthest away from the shit happening. We spread accountability like fertilizer. We sacrifice the accolades due for a spark of inspiration to the fear of it not working. Even when we're confident it will. We gather co-conspirators for our idea such that we can be happy co-defendants at the inquest into why it failed. "They can't fire us all." Except they might. In some places they think nothing of it. So, we bury the idea along with all the others and say no more of it until it later emerges, surgically drawn like a needle out of time, to help us regret we once buried it. But we're safe, for now. And safety always has a premium.

What of those doing what they love? The mantra has become the modern equivalent of the Athena[2] poster. For a tiny minority, a genuine reality. Some consider their work as a "calling" and it becomes their identity. Those working in their communities. Those working with wildlife or in the forest. Musicians whose songs we sing in the shower. Surgeons, piecing our bodies back together. It's rare because our reality is so often superficially imposed by the machinery of work and we may never know what we're truly "here to do." We become over-domesticated, written into tidy job descriptions in the name of efficiency by other over-domesticated beings. No place for the sentient.

Stress and tension are proportional. The sportsperson runs

on limited time. The naturalist is at the mercy of the climate emergency. Very often passion exacts a price, a share of the rewards that ought to be due. Which adds its own pressure. The suntanned, super-fit swimming coach we see in summer is in perilous debt. They're paid bugger all, their work is seasonal, and we think they're over-officious nags until they save our life. Their joints ache from the relentless training but they can't tell anyone. Just like we don't tell anyone, we put our headphones on and lower our gaze, dissolving into the blue light.

Yet, who is to say that we can't find our calling even in what appears to be the most menial work? A delivery driver who loses themselves in podcasts exploring the genius of classical composers, spending 6 hours a day believing the cabin of the van to be the orchestra pit, humming Holst as the package is hidden behind the plant pot by the front door as we sit beyond the hallway in silence tracing the error in a spreadsheet. We may believe their work is incidental to their passion, but they've grafted providing a vital service onto a love of something that co-exists with their paid labor. And when that role is automated, they become the host of an online education program on creating artful music, a sublime charm discernible in their colloquial appreciation of "high" (cost) art. And we still haven't found the error in our sheet.

Everyone is talent. "Talent" isn't a subset of us. Everyone deserves a world of work that's fair, supportive, developmental, caring, honest and rich in opportunity. Absolutely everyone. The only deviants, reprobates, arseholes and egotists – regular collegiate terms of disaffection – are those suppressed by their environment, organization, manager or even coworkers. People labeled as misfits who really are trying their hardest to make good in an industrial compactor of politics, power and abuse. A machine that has ensured many a Hendrix has withered in the post room, a Tolkien stagnated as a staff writer, an Arden plateaued as a junior HR Manager.

All too often the solution to perceived deficits in ability, flagging energy, distracted morale, even changing social norms, is training. We train for obedience, method, rules, protocols and we call the acquired acquiescence and techniques "skills." When our puppy learns it has to stick its paw in the air to get a treat, we don't call it a skill. But it's still prompt/action/reward. We put baristas through punishing bias training instead of providing resources and opening conversations to help them understand difference. Rather than stoking curiosity, which fuels further curiosity, we pile on competency. Which ends right there. Until the next time.

None of this was supposed to happen, of course. When organizations were assembled from the loose kit of catalog parts, they were well intentioned. They were going to right something, make something better, do something no-one had done before, make a difference and create wealth and better lives. They had clarity, desire, purpose. Even, on occasions, a destiny. They expressed a desire to gather the most able people, to give them a path, to treat them respectfully, to ensure they could actualize their own individual dream in the service of the collective. They meant it, too, in an honesty that was visible and tangible.

How did we get here? It's all been a terrible accident. We believe no-one ever meant it. That may seem naive at first. But no-one ever set out to do this. What they have done, rather, is unknowingly and unwittingly woven their stories into what it is today. It's marginal gains in reverse. Marginal drains, perhaps. A fatberg of planetary proportions. An accumulated mishap that has then become too much for anyone to even remotely begin to dismantle however many tracts they've sold or awards they've won. As collaborators on this book, we've added to it as well. We'd be horrified to see our own contribution, but it'll be in there somewhere, meshed, entwined. It's by no means just the "system" at fault. Many of us are inculcating, exploiting and hiding behind it. Occasionally or perpetually. We're the system as well as victims of it. It doesn't exist without us all. We're not stuck in a traffic jam, we *are* traffic.

So, we're here and we have to un-fuck work. This is where the profanity makes way – well, not entirely – for dismantling the structures, processes and myths that have led us to this point. Those we're within. And breaking the structures, processes and myths of *us*. As intimated in the introduction, this isn't a self-help book. It doesn't offer you a 10-step plan or a methodology or a snappy acronym you can tattoo on your backside. Or someone else's. Neither is it a trust-funded gap-year kick. The creators of this book have worked for decades in the fug, part-surviving it, always wanting to do something about it, doing what they can about it.

Rather, it's a liberation. A step toward a bearable lightness of work. A tale of optimism and hope, beyond the soporific memes on which we've become reliant. Belief in us. We've been pacified for long enough. We'll be left with fragments, shapes, ideas that we'll be able to assemble as we need. The creation will be dynamic. Sometimes the pieces will fit, sometimes they'll need to be re-assembled as our environment evolves. We can't tell yet how to do this and we can't assume the arrogance to believe we can. What can be fashioned is the understanding and energy to create work as we want it to be. Not in the way it's unforgivingly pumped into us from the first pointless, diminishing 5-minute school-leaver's conversation with a careers adviser. It's not naive, though. Stuff has to get done. The proposition blends asks, chores and activities with learning, discovery, advancement, growth and diversification.

Freedom is, after all, terrifying. The inevitability we conveniently held accountable for all the things we didn't think we could do has withered, leaving just us. In an empty room. With it all to build. But uncertainty – the core of innovation and creativity that organizations are designed to eradicate, to crush – is our opportunity. It's terrifying too because it's rare. So, when we taste it, it's often fascinatingly unfamiliar.

Un-fucked working is an awakening. We might call it re-wilding. Un-domestication. Like the husky that doesn't know it can run with a pack unless it's untethered. After feeling that sense of emancipation and self-determination, pulling a human and their sled and getting chained to a small kennel and fed on gristle just seems – well, fucked. It's not just about us. As the Iroquois Nation is famously denoted for its "seven generations" decision-making, where that which we determine today should benefit those seven generations into the future, so should our endeavor address both our present and the future for others, freeing they and ourselves from mere financial viability.

Over the next couple of hours, it will begin to feel like the most natural thing we've ever encountered. At which point work will, too. We'll want to do it. We'll do it better. We'll be better to be with and give more back. We'll still make mistakes and do and say the wrong thing and make bad calls. That inevitable human quality of being a bit of an arse will never go away. Because if it did, no-one would believe it's us.

We're going to un-fuck work. Fix it for good. For all time.

Chapter 2

"Work is something we do, not a place we go"

But it's not just that. Is it?

Humans have always worked. Even if, like the other creatures with which we shared the forests and plains for tens of thousands of years without much happening of note, to survive. When we fashioned spears from twigs and recorded our endeavors on cave walls with pre-Pantone squashed berries, we probably didn't have much of a conceptual idea of work. We just got on with it because we fundamentally had to. Our paintings recorded the doing, rather than the reason why. Life's got a shade more sophisticated since.

We're not going to get stuck into the history of work – we all know the journey from caves to fields to workshops to factories to inadvertently being on mute. Safe to say, however, that we should remember for many centuries manual work was regarded as punishment, something performed by slaves. Hebrew texts depict work as a "curse devised by God explicitly to punish the disobedience and ingratitude of Adam and Eve." Indeed, Rome wouldn't have been the all-conquering empire without the degrading toil of those who were bought and sold for the purpose of doing stuff so their owners could spend their time chewing the philosophical cud with their fellow elite. The toga didn't prove itself useful for manual labor.

What is work?

Answering this question is a little tricky, but necessary. We'll skip the suspense, it's three things: action, creation and location.

11

The opening statement, of unknown origin but now ubiquitous, misleadingly gives us a single meaning, action. So, we'll start with it.

Work is something we do. It is the engagement in mental or physical activity to make something happen. Whether paid or not, meaningful or fulfilling or not, we do it.

At a point in our evolution, the reason we worked morphed from simply wanting to see tomorrow – eat or be eaten – into more considered drivers, as we sought not just to respond to our world but to shape and understand it. We still tend to regard work as employment – working for gain, such is the necessity for most – but it extends way beyond, taking in all our physical and mental engagement. Fetching water, cooking, singing a lullaby, it's all work. It's always been something we do. That part of the opening statement is entirely true, but it's not enough.

Second, work is creation. It's what we leave behind, the residue of our labor. It can be tangible or intangible, noticed or unnoticed. It can be active (something) or passive (the absence of something). It's often considered to be simply our output, but it's far more; it's about the contribution we make, the outcome. While it can be rivets, it may just as likely be advice, mentoring, guidance, support, encouragement, care, or freely given assistance. When we've finished working, something is different. Whatever we do, it's inherently creative.

Unfortunately, creation gets confused with productivity, defined as output per unit of input. We're rather obsessed with the latter, locked as we still are in Industrial Age thinking, and nowhere near obsessed enough with the former. If I'm a security guard protecting a building at night, I'm creating confidence. There's no output, but there's an outcome.

That's not to forget that post-WWII as processes elongated and became more complex and the product of individual labor became more difficult to quantify, the shift began toward judging performance on what could be most easily (for which, read lazily) ascertained – input. The extent to which we were present, seen and heard. We could be abysmal at our work, but we were visible and audible. The idea has a very long tail.

Third and finally, its location. It can either be a location of intent, as in, a place we specifically go for the action and creation that is work, or a place we happen to be where work is possible. It is the contention surrounding this aspect of work that fuels the opening statement of this chapter.

During the Industrial Revolution, where we first began to "go to work" in numbers, the scale of the machinery on which we toiled meant we had to visit the mountain, it wasn't able to come to us. With the rise of "telecommuting," a phrase first gifted us by Jack Nilles with his experiments in corporate home working and his 1976 book *The Telecommunications-Transportation Tradeoff*[3], we're now able to challenge the notion that work is a destination of necessity. By 1989, Peter Drucker was declaring in a *Wall Street Journal* article that "commuting to office work is obsolete.[4]" Which it wasn't at the time, and for some time thereafter. We also now have the idea of "wirk" – work that's sourced, performed and paid for online, such that those involved at either end of the transaction never actually get to know how tall the other is unless they specifically ask. Which feels intrusive.

Of course, we physically have to *be somewhere* to work, but while in our own physical space can connect with others virtually, using digital communication tools. The argument about the quality of such interaction, and long-term implications for humanity, rages softly on similarly ethereal social channels. Media Richness Theory (MRT)[5] suggests that face-to-face communication is the most complete form of communication, yet we are led to wonder whether completeness is necessary when ranked against the breadth of access the digital workplace offers.

For many occupations, even attempting to separate work and place would create a logical absurdity. A bus driver needs a public service vehicle, a chef needs a kitchen, a shop assistant needs a retail outlet that hasn't been forced into liquidation from the rapid rise of online consumerism. It's not just a class divide, a collar color distinction. Take heftily-remunerated and well-educated surgeons, judges, restauranteurs – their roles are all as much defined by location as action and creation.

Class does come into it. The debate – or, rather, the self-reinforcing monologue – around placelessness is dominated by "ever-changing, dynamic, and autonomous" latte-sipping laptop-wielding "knowledge workers." Like us, probably. This genre, originally identified in 1959 by (wait for it, roll on the drums) Peter Drucker in *The Landmarks of Tomorrow*[6] as those whose labor would be mental rather than physical, represent a subset (office-ready workers) of a subset (those in paid employment) of the total working-age population (usually 16-64 years) which in the UK is just over 32 million[7] people.

Establishing the number of knowledge workers is tricky as no national data collection exercises in the UK or US segregate roles in such a manner. We do know, however, from UK government data that 47 percent of those in employment are in managerial, professional and associate professional/technical jobs.[8] As a further sub-set of this sub-set, around 10-11 million in the UK might be, within reason, a workable estimate. Roughly a third. A minority, but a vocal and powerful one that tends to believe that what applies to them applies to everyone. Not just collectively, but individually: "I like working from home" therefore we all like working from home.

The author of, and collaborators on, this book have had to face and accept their unfortunate contribution to this reality. We'll consider shortly how this intellectual energy can be put to far more beneficial use than sustaining the echo chamber in which it's locked.

Post the Covid-19 pandemic of 2020-21, with the scent of freedom and flexibility in the nostrils of those millions and the emergence from perceived eccentricity of location-agnostic organizations, we're reminded of some earlier dramatic disappointments. Whether Marissa Meyer's infamous edict to remote-working Yahoo staff in 2013[9] to return to the office for more "hallway and cafeteria discussions" or barely a week later Best Buy's abandonment[10] of its much-heralded "Results Only Work Environment" (ROWE) scheme that had been running since 2004, or IBM's "time's-up" klaxon for thousands of the 40 percent of its 386,000 employees in 173 countries[11] working at home or locally. We witnessed tech-fired tech-creating organizations in the throes of the tech age, returning to analog-centric notions, practices and anxieties.

Alongside the physical and virtual, location has a further component that reinforces the necessity for it to be retained in defining work: community. The assertion will surface on a number of occasions throughout this book, but no-one works entirely alone. Community is the ever-shifting human landscape in which we operate, broad and deep, irrespective of physical place or mode of communication. It gives us the entire rich experience, complete with room for the surprising and unexpected. When we work, acting and creating, we enter this sphere as we might through a physical door, "a place of allure," of the gravitational force of beauty and fascination as Charles Handy wrote while casting a slightly eccentric picture, ironically enough, of his ideal office.[12] Perhaps because it is the presence of people that transforms *space* into *place*.

Without community we face the brutal prospect of social anemia. The ease and reach of the virtual, for those able to work anywhere, is beguiling. Yet with every flat interaction we're reminded of the need to balance its easy charm with the physical – cologne, breath and glint – to ensure the health and vibrancy of community. For if not, it's loss will only make itself apparent long after it's dissolved. Through prolonged voluntary dispersal we'll no longer carry oxygen to the organization's tissue. It'll weaken and tire, and this in turn will deplete and exhaust us. The investment is ours to make.

Meaning and purpose

Most work has a purpose, even if it's ludicrous. A reason it's done. Someone decided something needed doing and so did it or found someone to do it. There's nothing fundamentally wrong with stating and understanding it, however. It helps us to connect dots. Its absence can be entirely disconcerting. We're reminded of Smallcreep, the pulley operator who, as the protagonist of Peter Currell Brown's acid-trippy novel[13], decides to explore the extent of the factory in which he works to understand where his task fits into the schema. It's an unfathomable, psychedelic world of surreal chaos. It has the same frustrating sense as Franz Kafka's unfinished novel *The Castle*[14] in which the closer we appear to be getting to an understanding of why the Land Surveyor was contracted, and to some actual work, the further away we actually get.

This is well beyond the condescending "common purpose" and "shared vision" myth – that to this day prompts spontaneous management consultant flagellation – of a janitor in 1962 at Cape Canaveral proudly informing the visiting President Kennedy that he was "helping put a man on the moon." The story is ridiculous for a number of reasons and a glaring expression of white male privilege. But what happened to our mythical wage laborer? He kept sweeping the floors, being treated like the dirt in his scoop, until being laid off the moment the Apollo 11 command module Columbia broke the swell of the Atlantic in July 1969 to raptures across the globe. He didn't watch the splashdown as he didn't have a television, nor did anyone he knew. Nobody thanked him for helping.

Meaning goes a step further. It tells us something that's not directly expressed. It doesn't just say we need to bash a rivet into a panel so that the assembler can then install it in the machine. It helps us see our rivet as an essential component of the whole, without which the entirety wouldn't be possible, and value or enjoyment wouldn't be derived by the user. The organization could kindly point that out to us, in which case we're informed, but when we find it out for ourselves the discovery is both enlightening and satisfying. Either way, meaning is derived. As a result, our work matters to us. Yet it's not that easy.

Many of the consequential ills of the rapid, unstoppable and (in his view) inevitable rise of capitalism in the eighteenth and nineteenth centuries that we tangle with today were foremost in the thought and work of Karl Marx, informed by his ethnographer sidekick Friedrich Engels. Politically discredited today for all but the purist, his analytical frameworks remain highly useful.

Marx's thinking in this regard centered on our alienation from our humanity, the cause of which was the capitalist means of production. Marx concluded in his *Economic and Philosophic Manuscripts* of 1844 that there were four strands (the bracketed text added for clarity).[15] First, from our output (what we do). As we're not making stuff directly, there's nothing of "us" in it. Second, the process of producing stuff (how we do it). We have to do it rather than choose to. Third, from our colleagues (who we do it with), as it's a perpetual and brutal scrap over higher pay. Finally, from ourselves (what it does to us), as we lose control of shaping our lives. It reads like a gentle Saturday late-morning scroll through LinkedIn.

Time has healed three of these strands. We've somewhat resolved our alienation from our output through reconciling ourselves to it. The knowledge economy has brought us closer once again to the product of our labor than the satanic mills allowed. The iron fist of coercion now wears a designer cashmere glove (velvet being a little too Napoleonic) and exudes the

17

calm of a podcaster. As promising as that sounds, instead of merely shafting one another for an extra shilling a week, we manage to find new ways to disengage from our colleagues while celebrating the very freedom to do so. Some *have* even celebrated it. Julia Hobsbawm's pamphlet for the think-tank Demos (and soon to be book) is entitled the *Nowhere Office*, as though despite the intended irony in the title, such a soulless dispersal may even be considered aspirational.[16]

Of the fourth, in the midst of this disconnection therefore we strive to relate to our work, in even some small way, in order to repair this divide between ourselves and our labor, to regain control. Whose responsibility is that? The organization, to create work to which we can relate – or our own, to ascribe meaning, even if as an artifice?

Even for those doing what they love or responding to a metaphysical calling, to which we referred in Chapter 1 and for whom the meaning in their work isn't in question, their labor may not be without its pitfalls. A football reporter likely adores the beautiful game, even though they may curse their car breaking down just past midnight on a darkened stretch of motorway a hundred miles from home on a freezing December evening after struggling to find anything worth saying about a tedious mid-table nil-nil draw. Many more will grow to enjoy work they never thought they would find meaning in until trying it. The driver of the attending breakdown vehicle has come to appreciate the open road, variable hours, people interaction, the sense of performing a valued and necessary service and the library of stories they have to tell. His colleague, meanwhile, hates it and can't wait to sack it off. She wants to be a football reporter.

Yet this is all paid work. The majority of the burden of unpaid work – childcare and household activities – falls on women. A whopping 60 percent of it according to the Office for National Statistics[17] in the UK. In rural communities in the developing world this extends to farming, too, plowing a field of baked earth being a natural step from the washing up. Globally women spend 4.5 hours a day on unpaid work, more than double that of men according to OECD data.[18] Yet while we're straining to discern a shred of meaning in a routine accounts payable processing role, we don't hear any call for it in the mire of daily chores, that's just considered the shit we have to get done regardless.

Meaning in work can – and should be – universal. Wherever, whenever, whoever. Paid or unpaid. However distant from the eventual product or outcome. Adored or detested. As long as it needs doing, as a critical test, it can mean something to us. And it won't need a click-bait feature article to give us the ten tips on how. We'll get to the gender imbalance shortly – that's not slipping through the fuckery dragnet.

Undefining work

The opening statement presents a problem to us in several additional respects. First, the privilege of the knowledge worker we identified earlier. We're those freed from the drudgery of process tedium, individually portable enough to work wherever the regime or fancy leads us. It's no coincidence that we're the lifeblood of professional social networks. It's a self-perpetuating indifference to the reality experienced by many. If we were to drill into the educational, gender and ethnic profiles of such a cohort, we'd be unlikely to find it even grazing an organization's equality and inclusion targets.

Yet being a knowledge worker often hides a story. We're not all born into the genre, Montblanc in our mouth. Many of us within the bracket have worked our way to a situation of comfort, traversing every chapter in this book. We've taken what we believe to be right from our experience and found soul in our work. We've guided others wherever we've been able and watched as those who haven't found our ways to their liking drift in other directions.

Second, in this regard it's also a continuation of the atomization of work, a product of the re-emergence and political embrace of individualism in the late 1980s with the economic thought of Friedrich Hayek and his contemporaries. It played to the original tenet of liberalism that holds that as long as our free choices don't harm others than they take precedence over the interests of the collective. It has a tricky history with multiple interwoven threads, yet Max Stirner stands out for offering the ultimate statement of unmitigated self-determination in his 1844 work *The Ego and its Own*.[19] He paints the ego not just as the middle-aged white male in the double-aspect corner office but us all, driven by innate personal autonomy. The Covid-19 pandemic has, through our social isolation, inevitably once again turned our focus onto ourselves and our personal interests. Our "ownness," as Stirner calls it, is an ever-present idea.

Of course, the workplace is littered daily with the detritus of ego conflict. Almost no-one works alone, however weak or occasional the ties. Even a lighthouse keeper needs supplies, the guiding light a program of preventive maintenance. Which means all work is in some way connected. Work is by its very nature a community, dysfunctional though it may appear. The centrifugal force of individual free choice pushes against our innate togetherness, but dependency prevents it from breaking away. We therefore have to consider the "place we go" to work in the abstract as well as the tangible, comprising all those with whom we're associated in our work, whether we know them or not. Our choices – and our acts and omissions – have consequences for those with whom we work, as theirs do for us.

It may be hard to consider when we're in the midst of a difficult annual appraisal where our contribution to a team effort is being ritually dissected, but it's not all about us. We don't say, "a drink is something you consume, not a place you go." We can buy a take-home from an off license and guzzle it alone or with friends. But the act of "going for a drink" implies a venue, the company of others we value (or may grow to), a period of time and the potential for something unexpected. We picture an entire positive experience. The same is true of the workplace. Particularly regarding the unexpected when over half of people admit to having had a romantic relationship with a colleague.[20] Perhaps for a fair percentage of the remainder, not for the want of imagining or trying.

Third and finally, it's ridiculously and needlessly confusing. Humans are pattern-seeking creatures. We have to make around 35,000 decisions every day.[21] If we can nail the most regular and rudimentary, it frees our mind for more interesting pursuits. Or endless scrolling on a smartphone. Of course, this is always highlighted in the habits of business founders (usually male) but that's only due to their media profile. "Did you hear? Billy Bigballs only wears two outfits all week. All that money, too."

Choice adds layers of decisions to an already oversold day. It's glorification neglects to identify this in the terms and conditions. Establishing a regular physical place of work, wherever that may be, creates a pattern-forming convenience. All the other parallel facets of life operate to such patterns too, such as schools, shops and entertainment. Yet the opposite – free choice – is touted as a non-negotiable beneficial contributor to our wellbeing. Most occupants of what have been termed "agile" workplaces, which are, of course, offices, with lots of different shared settings for the different things we do all day (which aren't actually that different), don't care for or seek to understand the underlying philosophy of the space, they just want somewhere to sit. So, grappling with the freedom gifted by work no longer being a place we go is, for most, just another monumental pain in the backside. Which is why it suits the well-educated, middle-class knowledge worker and virtually no-one else.

Un-f✱cking the meaning of work

Our unrequited love of the binary is in this regard – work having to be either a place we go *or* something we do – misplaced, and generates a host of negative consequences. In order to mitigate or avoid such, our statement therefore becomes:

"~~Work is something we do, not a place we go~~"

"Work is something we do, something we create and a place we are"

We're actively involved in something that has an effect, outcome or product – it yields something, for a reason. In doing so we're somewhere – in a physical space, of whatever form, and a community, however transient: it's not always a place we go, but somewhere in both respects we are at a point in time. This will change throughout a typical day and evolve at a broader level over time. We're never nowhere.

There are three emergent keys to un-fucking this most frivolous of propositions, with all the chaos it brings to our work, and seeing it as re-stated.

First, we must always be aware of our privilege and learn to see working life as others might. The angle from which we observe the rest of working society will invariably be elevated. From here we'll see everyone living and toiling as we see ourselves, imposing our reality on them. Yet what work means to us isn't what it will mean to many. Further, behaving in a privileged way only serves to drive destructive division and resentment. Knowledge workers are, and will remain, a minority whatever all those economists laid end-to-end will conclude about post-technological pursuits. And robots. Our collective duty is to improve the lot of those who don't have the luxury of our choices. It's high time we understood and started to do so.

Second, rather than dismissing it as no longer relevant we

must value "place" in its broadest sense as both a physical and collective experience, the energy of community, a vital counter to our historic struggle with alienation. The mistake we've always made with the idea is to consider it in purely tangible terms – the production line, the laboratory, the rows of white desks. If in our pursuit of self-determination we find ourselves distanced from what we do, how we do it, who we do it with and what it does to us, the community is our recourse, our reminder of why we do it at all. It's where we begin and to where we return.

Finally, all work should be needed, and therefore none should go without meaning. In this sense, its meaning is universal. It's not a case of either/or, or a question of degree. Sometimes work is needed to prove that it's not needed, to close off an avenue. That's fine, as long as only as much is undertaken to establish so. If it's not needed, we should speak up and be heard, such that we can stop doing it and do something that's needed instead. There will always be an element of work in this category, caught in the time lag between identification and removal, yet it should never be allowed to stagnate while it's identified. Which means we're always evaluating the need. In this sense labor can be a leveler, a generator and driver of dignity. Completing every story.

Leaving no-one behind.

Chapter 3

"Hard work never hurt anyone"

Yet it did. Didn't it?

Because so said a survivor. Survival doesn't come in shades – it's binary.

Consider "whelm," a curiosity of the English language. It means to engulf or bury, its Anglo-Saxon roots suggesting to submerge. But we never hear it spoken. We hear "overwhelmed" when we're immersed or entombed – or starting to feel this way – or "underwhelmed" when we're unimpressed, nonplussed, when an impact hasn't been made upon us. There's no middle ground, no neutral position.

So it is with work.

We're either on top of it or underneath it. The reward for being on top of it is more of it until we're underneath it. Unless we keep quiet about it. But "busyness" has become a badge of honor, instant self-validation. That's where we're compliant, grateful for small mercies. Fearful of our own idle, wandering thoughts, we're willingly careless with what we wish for. Until the weeds wrap around our ankles, the light fades, the grassy banks empty, and we're alone.

At various times in our working lives, we've sat in the workplace, as colleagues have thoroughly and begrudgingly complied with the housekeeping mandate and cursed the bastard that made the miserable evening of toil stretching out before us inevitable. We've fancifully toyed at that moment with the idea of taking the offending requirement somewhere more congenial. We've sat among those on the late train home who, judging by their exuberance, clearly weren't faced with any such dilemma. We're convinced Excel must have burned off the surface of our corneas, for the streetlights starburst. And when home, we remove the packaging and pierce the film, accepting the indigestion to follow as a necessary inconvenience.

We've all recognized during our career, sometimes for prolonged periods, that working late into the evening is part of the informal contract, if not part of the formal. The stuff that gets us noticed, even if at times only by the excellent cleaning team who've usually already finished a day's work elsewhere and look upon our predicament with envy. Or all weekend. Or through dinner, or a date, or the mythical "quality time" with our children, or an entire holiday. Or in the diminutive hours when we're composing emails in our head. Or actual emails on our mobile phone, our face glowing in the gloom. Or simply indulging in that familiar therapeutic pastime of playing out the full fuck-you fuck-off consequence-free resignation in front of the entire company and all its extended shareholders and anyone who has ever heard of it. We fall asleep moments before the alarm.

How hard is hard?

Stressed, anxious, overwhelmed. Without doubt, words in increasingly frequent usage. The broken backs of the industrial and extraction age have become the splintered spirits of modernity. The injuries to our forebears were sudden, visible and terrible, the screams ear-splitting. More than this, they were potentially cataclysmic. Survival often meant a slower demise through an inability to work with a safety net, at the time considered an extreme radical curiosity. Emile Zola's 1877 novel L'Assommoir[22] tracks the dark descent into alcoholism and poverty of the once-teetotal Coupeau following a fall from the roof he was constructing. He drags his wife Gervaise into the chasm with him, drink by drink. Those who went before might consider us to be pathetic at best. We breathe fresh air. We're warm. Our injuries are slow, invisible and often questionable.

The screams personal, silent, festering, accumulating. We can pass quietly into dust, and no-one will be any the wiser.

Remarkably, it was Philip II of Spain in 1593 who blazed the trail for humane labor, establishing an 8-hour work day by a royal edict known as "Ordenanzas de Felipe II," dividing the day into two 4-hour stints.[23] It was designed not only to maximize productivity but, for those laboring, "attended to ensure their health and conservation." Wellbeing isn't a new idea.

During the Industrial Revolution the 10-16 hour day, 6 days a week was commonplace. Every day was "bring your child to work" day. It was in some instances compulsory. Robert Owen, founder of the experimental socialist community at New Lanark Mills in Scotland – a committed advocate of shorter workdays – coined the rally slogan: "Eight hours labor, eight hours recreation, eight hours rest" in 1817. It was the start of a hundred-year campaign. In 1926, Ford in the US was the first to enact it at scale, along with a pay rise. Productivity increased. In a world where for office-based workers the hard-won "9-5" feels anachronistic when we're able (and sometimes permitted) through the use of mobile technology to work when, where and how we choose, for many in less fortunate parts of the world the "9-5" and a 5-day week remain a distant hope. Necessary and welcome progress as it is for some, we forget quite what a struggle it was to attain it and how fortunate we are to be in a position to mock it.

A study published in 2021 by the World Health Organisation (WHO) and International Labor Organisation (ILO) concludes that working 55+ hours a week – to which 9 percent of the total population are subject – creates a 35 percent higher risk of stroke and 17 percent higher risk of dying from heart disease compared to a 35-40 hour week.[24] It bites later in life, mostly affecting those 60-79 years old.

Graham Greene's 1960 novel about a doctor treating leprosy patients in the Belgian Congo, *A Burnt Out Case*[25], gifted us the term in the title that we find in liberal use today. The mere thought of the assignment would have brought on many of the attributed symptoms – physical and mental exhaustion, alienation, anomie, anger, cynicism and a need for constant validation – while we searched for our passport. Burnout is effectively a state where stress and anxiety have won.

When the WHO recognized the condition in 2019 it used the Maslach Burnout Inventory (MBI) as its framework, developed in 1981 by Christina Maslach, with six risk categories: workload, sense of control, reward, workplace relationships, fairness and values alignment. Unsurprisingly, much of the content of this book. Yet we struggle with determining the origin and factors that exacerbate it in an individual, and with its diagnosis given that the symptoms and their severity are subjective; the MBI is a 10-minute self-assessment questionnaire. Nevertheless, it often manifests as something we recognize in others even if they fail to see it in themselves.

Collaborator on this book Perry Timms argues in his book *The Energized Workplace*[26] that there's a finite stock of kilojoules available in the human battery to cope with a working day, and that we had already reached "peak work" even before the first signs of the Covid-19 pandemic. With the addition of the risk or actuality of being ill and losing loved ones, social isolation, home-schooling and trying to keep a job or business alive, we're using more than we can sustain every day. The stock is never replenished, and it begins to drain the energy that's needed for other essential functions of the mind and body.

The Japanese have a word for working oneself to death – "karoshi." Either this is surprising or it's surprising that no-one else seems to. Who's right? Most of us will have experienced those in the workplace who, no matter how early we get in, are there before us, or how late we leave are still bathed in fluorescence as we get our coat. Whether their elastic presence is driven by acute loneliness, playground machismo, incompetence or a total inability to manage their workload, we're always on a half day by comparison. Sometimes they even kindly remind us, with a hint of egotistical or involuntary glib. The Japanese office worker's average of 2000 hours' work a year, however, is only an hour a week longer than that in the UK.[27] They just have a word for it.

Perhaps the lack of an English karoshi is down to the expression "mustn't grumble" which one commentator assures us was "one of the principles on which British civilization was founded."[28] Within the toolkit of exceptionalism, it provides a ready-made shrug to any hardship, however oppressive or threatening. It's a casual derivative of the more formal demonstration of resolve, the "stiff upper lip," which actually originated with the emotionally anemic Spartans in Ancient Greece only to be later purloined by the equally emotionally anemic but far more entitled British public school system that has forever beget the political and administrative among us. Or even for the pampered corporate male of any domicile, it represents a resilience in the face of adversity that demands they "man up,"[29] the ultimate expression of withered virility. In whatever form, and wherever located, the sense that things that happen there won't happen here silently stalks the post-watershed workplace. Hard work won't hurt us.

At least it won't hurt us men. Only it does – the same WHO/ILO study (2021) showed men accounted for 72 percent of deaths from longer working hours. There's no female equivalent to this stubbornness, fortunately. Most women aren't burdened by this fragile, self-imposed emotional constriction, which far better equips them for the rigors of corporate life. Even so, the expression of emotion – by women – is still regrettably deemed a weakness, despite being a human, not a gender, response. As we'll explore in Chapter 6, just about everything else is stacked against women. Placing men in the unequal position of women, with their depleted ability to navigate it, would have relegated them to also-rans millennia ago.

When we're talking "hard work," of course, we mean varying shades of "hard." Frederick Taylor, scourge of the leisured classes, writing in the 1920s believed that workers were naturally lazy and when working in groups would default to the level of output of the slowest among them. The weakest link as role model. This tendency he called "natural soldiering" – taking it easy. Inevitably, a masculine expression. In this regard workers would look after their own wellbeing, an age before the corporation began playing parent (but several centuries after Philip II), and saw no benefit in what has become known in recent times as "discretionary effort" (or the more palatable "above and beyond") unless it was remunerated. Taylor's solution comprised both stick (constant supervision) and carrot (payment linked to output). The lack of nuance in this analysis is striking to us today, but a Taylorist underbelly lurks in many a workplace culture, even if not readily admitted. Scratch-and-sniff to reveal your own.

How hard are we talking, therefore? Properly hard. In the modern workplace we expect a certain degree of challenge in a role – deadlines, problems, innovations, projects, budgets and management. They even have a motivating effect as we battle against our own assessment of our capabilities. We've come to accept that, fundamentally, work isn't supposed to be easy. What we're addressing here is where it's excessive over a significant period of time, whether in regard to management, resources, difficulty, disorganization, unpredictability or strategy. Or all of the above. Shortage of time is a symptom, not a cause.

Technology often gets the blame for excessive work, even though it's enabled us to be potentially significantly more productive too. It provides the means (mobile and connected kit and applications), motive (to either catch up or get ahead) and opportunity (we can work almost anywhere). Of course, we can always leave it alone or put it down, just as a committed smoker can stub it out and omit lighting another. There's still some debate as to whether technology can be addictive, albeit the WHO have thus far only listed Internet Gaming Disorder as a disease. Yet the insatiable urge to scroll, the dopamine-seeking reward loop, snares us, dangling the promise of fulfillment just out of reach. Technology has become both liberator and oppressor. When we're too engrossed to discern the difference, the oppressor has won.

There's also the matter of why we're working excessively. It could be the generic bastard we referred to in the opening paragraph. The one who made us do it, leaving us no alternative but insubordination or exit. It could, of course, be us. We're often complicit. Perhaps we take on more than we should to show willing, or to prove ourselves, or to be able to hold work responsible for our not taking our chances because it's easier than facing our own self-doubt. Maybe we're simply not very good at what we're doing, having left a little too much headroom in taking on the role, puffed up our experience a little too much. We may have a misplaced sense of obligation, an altogether imaginary voice that tells us we ought to be doing it, a self-generating guilt. Or we're lonely and have nothing we want to do so we just work because it has a specificity that brings rigor, structure and purpose to our otherwise empty lives. Of course, we're not ruling out that we may either believe it needs doing for a greater good, or that we simply enjoy it.

They're the candidates for motivation – but what in heaven's name, then, are we doing? It's become lost in the endless timeline but somewhere on Twitter it was written that "95 percent of work is noise." That may be a slight overestimation, but it would be almost disrespectful not to mention "Parkinson's Law[30]" at this point: "Work expands so as to fill the time available for its completion." The idea that time, the scarcest resource, is the ultimate arbiter of what we do remains compelling even in the asynchronous world of work where we're not all in the same physical place together. It's Dante's nine concentric circles of hell spewing tasks that pass between us without end. Work that generates work that's unable to break from the cycle. It's known in legal corridors that practitioners of the craft greet one another with "are you busy?" in full recognition that activity precedes health. When facing a computer screen, anyone can look busy, wherever they are. It's hiding in the plainest of sight.

However busy we are, or more accurately believe we are, unless there's a specific outcome – one of our three definitions of work we covered in the previous chapter – it's invisible. If we judge our productivity against getting through a list of stuff that's crap, then it's not productivity, it's actually crap. Yet somehow we and those who asked us to do it are happy.

How hurt is hurt?

The modern version of "hurt" comes in a variety of shades. From the momentary glancing blow that a wince sees off, to the long and almost imperceptible erosion of our dignity and our increasingly self-detrimental response in a vain attempt to cope. We don't have a measure, a graded scale, a meter on which we can check how we're doing and adjust accordingly. There's no real time read-out. We now strap digital bands on our wrists for clues, but the data still needs analyzing and contextualizing. The device checking our pulse and sleep patterns isn't going to warn us that another weekend of financial modeling is going to whip a further 6 months off our lives assuming that's where the intrusion ends. The human body has a remarkable knack of sending warning signs. The trouble is we ignore them or perceive them to be something else. We often only join the dots when it's too late. Or we don't join them at all and leave others to do so.

The most common modern symptom of excessively hard work has become stress. Its chronic, more serious form is anxiety. Yet "stress" somehow strikes a more disturbing chord, so we'll stick with it. The power of onomatopoeia. Stress is a term borrowed from physics, whereby a force exerts a strain on a subject. The first notable use in relation to ourselves was Hans Selye in Montreal in the 1920s while completing his medical training.[31] He noticed that humans released hormones when subjected to stress, which he termed the "General Adaptation Syndrome" (GAS) comprising: an alarm reaction where fight-or-flight is triggered; resistance, in which the body adapts by using resources intended for other important things; and exhaustion, where the immune system eventually can't take anymore and allows in all-comers. GAS. Released when stressed. It's hard to know if it's serious. But it is. Stressors can be both physiological or psychological, and either universal (for example, a tsunami or earthquake) or relative (particular to us). It's the psychological and relative stress that eats us alive from the workplace out. The UK's Health and Safety Executive (HSE) reported 17.9 million working days lost to stress, depression or anxiety in 2020. That's not far short of a day for each of the working population. They're just the ones lost. Many, of course, will be working on through theirs, accumulating as they go.

We're offered two traditional paths to dealing with stress: prevention and cure. As has become typical with the modern workplace, we're far more willing to tread the latter path to avoid having to deal with that which has become solidified, codified and institutionalized. Such a pattern will permeate this book, soaking through the pages, a shame on us all for collectively both allowing it to happen and believing that a gauze and tape is ever likely to be enough. Complexity is never a valid excuse. Even to consider the measures we take – dressed as is the fashion in the mockery of "wellbeing" programs – as a "cure" to any degree is to flatter ourselves and our efforts. They're anesthetics, the temporary relief from sensation. They attract armies of willing administrators to the cause of the corporate good. The problem being that in our own state of anesthesia, we're willing to believe that the plan is working, which perpetuates the avoidance of considering the cause.

The emergence of resilience has a lot to answer for, from simple coping techniques and mechanisms to a full psychological rebuild for the modern age. A healthy degree of this elixir is important, stemming from the days when it was a case of eat or be eaten. We're not starting from the base point of a blubbing, incapable and helpless mess. In the evolution of homo sapiens, however, we forget sometimes that the remarkable progress made from the Ancient Greeks to today represents around 1 percent of our time on the planet, and 0.1 percent from the Industrial Revolution to this very day. Our essentially Stone Age cognitive wiring retains some beneficial aspects in this regard, such as those features associated with self-preservation (the walnut-sized "fight-or-flight" amygdala, for example), and some problematic features, such as those associated with self-preservation. The rub being that the standard-issue emotional kit isn't too sophisticated when it comes to dealing with the subtleties of an excessive workload in a corporate snake pit.

Hence, we've developed a whole series of responses to help offset the pressure. From mindfulness (the irony of smartphone apps for this pursuit) and meditation to detoxification and dietary planning to exercise programs and competitive sport to sleep programs to flotation tanks. Of course, none of these are wrong in any shape or guise, nor to any rationale. We *should* be eating healthily, exercising regularly, taking time to clear our mind and sleeping like a new-born. All worthwhile as valid pursuits in themselves, not merely to be considered as antidotes to a whelmed existence.

We should simultaneously be avoiding the worst forms of reaction to another arbitrary deadline, such as drinking irresponsibly or indulging in recreational drugs ("I'm not addicted, I could stop if I wanted to…"). It's often not the stress itself that kills us; it's the responses it can drive us to. Yet this all comprises the use of lifestyle to offset the havoc wrought by work. It's more gawping through the wrong end of the telescope. Dealing with what we feel we can control. "Un-fuck work? Nah, I'll have a kale smoothie, face pack and an early night, and my boss might not be quite such an arse in the morning."

The damage done

So, while we're wondering if all that pulped vegetation makes a difference, what does hard work hurt?

First, in terms of simple opportunity cost, it erodes our personal relationships. Every choice to work at a time outside of the customary daylight-centered hours is potentially the rejection of another (night shifts are usually not a choice). And when we're finally done, it's our husk that greets them, the shreds that remain when the best of us has been gifted to the leviathan. We can, of course, pretend we're not "at work," when our gaze is distant, our pocketed smartphone gnawing into our thigh, and our attention on the tiny spaces fishing for our focus. The behavior is rarely called out before it's too late, when the lopsided ledger can't be redressed. It almost *has* to be too late to warrant it being mentioned in an age when it's verging on expected. Only the vacuum where our relationships used to be brings it home. A home, that is, we no longer share.

It slowly dismantles our sense of self-worth. With every oversized contribution our efforts are normalized. They become expected by our colleagues and remarked on if we don't achieve the levels we've established. It's what we do and how we do it. With each incremental task we're convinced we haven't quite worked hard enough because we haven't demonstrably nudged the bar higher, and that there was more we could have done. While we relish the praise for our efforts, another piece of Stone Age cerebral machinery, the habenula, wonders why the reward was smaller than we expected. "Is that all?" The response: to try harder, to prove to ourselves we're better than that. We thrive on a diet of disillusionment. No-one sees this in the same manner as us, so no-one checks in. We're left to deal with it alone.

It sets us apart. Convinced of our supreme commitment, we judge ourselves against our comparatively soldiering colleagues. Lazy bastards. Our tolerance of their inferior input progressively wanes, and precious relationships deteriorate. We take on tasks we should be passing to our team because we believe we can do them better and faster, and that delegation is a waste of precious time and energy when we could be getting on with it. We take on tasks that could be satisfactorily completed by our peers because they appear distracted or unconvinced. Our frame of reference distorts. We can no longer communicate with our team and peers as we see the path ahead so differently. We've separated.

Unintuitively, it can crush our chances of advancement. The very thing it's often being pursued in aid of. Our unrivaled reputation for grunt begins to appear almost primitive, unsophisticated. We're the jobbing, dependable slogger that allows others the space for freedom of expression. The hours we toil are a watery gray. Those noticed are the savvy shapers, the canny crafters, shrewd and insightful, with an impeccable sense of timing for their ideas and contribution. They couldn't operate without those creating the space for them to do so – us. Yet they don't realize it, it just appears to be the natural state of things, so thanks are rarely forthcoming. Their apparent idleness is overlooked in favor of their luminescence amid those monochrome hours. We curse those we enable, unaware of our complicity. When the effort reaps progressively less opportunity, nothing makes sense.

It makes us incalculably boring, salvation from which is a long and painful haul. It denies us the chance to pursue all the things that might create points of interest. Side hustles, hobbies, even the most normal of pursuits like film or sports or photographing the cat. No-one's expecting us to enrich our lives with wonder, just to offer a glimmer of fascination with something that doesn't involve budgets or programs. Something we can latch onto in conversation that involves an entirely personal and policy-free choice of attire and that creates a degree of commitment or passion. Because even on LinkedIn, no-one is interested in what time we get up in the morning, what we do when we do, what train we catch, what the station looks like under lights at 5am, what the other slaves to their own marginal gains are eating instead of breakfast, or why we value our commute as some form of sadistic interlude between the home we rarely see and the home we'd rather be in. To paraphrase a proverb that first appeared in James Howell's 1659 work *Proverbs*, all work and no play make Jack or Jill an utterly insufferable pillock. And quite possibly a virgin.

Finally, it damages the organization too. We're not here to give a flyer about the employing behemoth, but we'll dwell on the irony for a moment. The employment experience is just as any other in an age of instant, anonymous and universally accessible ratings. If we're happy, along with thousands of other lost yet houseproud souls, to leave a review of a carpet sweeper on a retail website, we'll sure as hell reveal the true character of our paymaster wherever we get the chance. As long as that all-important anonymity is assured, naturally. A reputation for effort that's more enforced than discretionary carries like a whisper on the Khamsin. Just as will an expectation of the discretionary grafters without an occasional acknowledgment in kind. Thanks, after all, don't pay the mortgage. Or fund the hobby that makes us really interesting to be with. The organization, happily thinking it's grinding out value from its unsuspecting charges, slowly sinks from the hairline cracks in its hull, blissfully unaware, until it bursts.

Un-f*cking the workload

All work needs to be appropriate to human capability, even

though our ability to perform it varies either wholly or by circumstance. It's vital that we know why we're doing what we do (we're just about to say more about purpose in the next chapter), that we have the means to do it, and where we find that we're struggling we have the means to identify so, with the expectation of remedial action without fear of reproach. That also means looking out for others too, who may not have found the confidence to speak, just as we hope others are doing for us. Sometimes we simply forget ourselves.

In establishing that relentless hard work is harmful – either for its direct impact or the damaging behavior it prompts in those affected – our statement becomes:

"~~Hard work never hurt anyone~~"

"We're driven by purpose – and know our limits in pursuing it"

If we have an ounce of energy left, there are three means to un-fuck the pursuit of exhaustion demanded by the cult of relentlessness.

First, we must stop seeing and considering excessive effort as a badge of honor in the workplace. Work must be balanced. The most important outcome from our labor, the source of its value, is our contribution. There may be certain roles for whom this is measured quantitatively, or particular aspects of our role, but for most, it's much more complex. There may be times where the contribution is extraordinary. But it's considered extraordinary for a reason – the necessity of its rarity. It's then both precious and appreciated, rather than taken for granted.

Second, if the unusually high workload for our colleagues has been necessitated by us, then we can alleviate the effects through showing appropriate gratitude. Unappreciated effort can be withering. Our response matters more than we can ever imagine. Recognition of the time and energy spent, and commitment shown, the offering of thanks and appreciation, and the granting of an appropriate concession, however small, can mean a huge amount. We hypothesized that the mythical cleaner at Cape Canaveral was never thanked after the moon landing, to illustrate that it would have been the hardest part of it all to take. Showing gratitude benefits both the receiver and giver, generating that most precious of commodities in both, optimism. We'll be prepared to commit again when needed, understanding that it's not the norm.

Finally, balance has a habit of tipping or being tipped. In this sense fairness is our barometer – judged objectively, observed continually, reviewed regularly, deviations acknowledged, and adjustments made willingly and for a shared beneficial outcome. This imposes a duty on us all, as managers and managed, peers and friends. Fairness faces in all directions at once. We have to *make* fairness. It must be enshrined in the formal systems of work, and alive, encouraged and fed within the informal. It requires proactive and reactive measures, setting standards and expectations, and responding quickly and overtly when they slip or aren't met. We can't expect that it's all something we're gifted, either. We reap what we sew in this regard. The fairer we are and are seen to be, the fairer will others be with us. This enables us to more easily speak up when we see or experience something that doesn't appear to be so.

Where this fairness dissolves or is abused, and its antithesis emerges, we must have the eyes to see and an open permission to intervene. That is, as with the manner in which fairness works, in all directions: up, down and sideways. We need to look out for our colleagues, to know and see the signs. We must immediately call out the imposition of impossible – even unreasonable – deadlines, the uneven distribution of tasks, conscious under-resourcing, thanklessness despite the effort, never allowing such behavior to settle. It's often the early indication of bullying, which we'll cover next. It has no place in the modern workplace. It never did in the old, we just accepted it.

When we witness our colleagues sending emails both before we've wiped the sleep from our eyes and when we're folding back the quilt; when their behavior turns on the unexpected, on their colleagues or on us; when we realize we're not within the focus of their thousand-yard stare; we intervene. As with the entirety of un-fucking work, we're not just involved, we're leading.

Chapter 4

"It's not a blame culture"

But we need to know whose fault it was. Don't we?

And if we don't know, or can't be sure, we'll make a convenient guess. Blame is an accusation. Something has gone wrong, and someone must be the cause. They did something they shouldn't have or didn't do something they should have. It gets apportioned regardless. Blame hates a void; it must be sated and quickly. At some point it's coming our way and it's thoroughly unpleasant, the double-decker tire tracks prove it. If it's correctly applied, we have three options – take it full on the chin, look to disperse it across circumstances or others, or both. If it's not, we can fight it or accept it. Washing it off isn't easy, blame is remarkably sticky.

In the workplace it's institutionalized, whether formally or informally. It serves two intrinsically related purposes: denigration and liberation. Through being apportioned to one or more people, it thereby sets the remainder free. It's emotive, amorphous, more likely to be liberally daubed than precision targeted. That bystanders are tarred is incidental. It's diminishing and entirely destructive. Fault, meanwhile, is in direct contrast rational, subject to enquiry and usually – it's hoped – based on evidence and free of confirmation bias. Fault is patient, it can await due process to ensure that it's correctly ascribed. The desired outcome is learning, to enable measures to be taken so that it doesn't happen again. That's not to say there isn't a better way still, as shall be explored. Blame merely demands that someone suffers and is seen to suffer. Even a little. That's where it ends.

The principal enabler and driver of a blame culture is the

method of organization that served the developed world so well for centuries in its relentless pursuit of the accumulation of wealth: command and control hierarchy. Almost all organization charts are still drawn to resemble its classic pyramid structure. We refer to "line management" as a means of designating the path of authority from the top to the bottom. Supposedly "flat" structures of which many like to lay claim are merely a variant, still a pyramid. They're a visual metaphor for order, the triangle as the most robust geometric shape offering comfort that it isn't going to fall apart or collapse. The top being smaller than the base means it can't compress under its own weight. It also comes with a heap of military jargon, given its roots. Like the "front line," being where once we faced an enemy and now it's an unsuspecting customer. Some still haven't noticed the transition. It's so ingrained, it's intuitive. We get it without having to think about it.

Within the structure, everyone is assigned responsibility. Our name and intended outcomes are entwined. Responsibility and accountability are used interchangeably, there's no need to try and differentiate for our purposes. They translate into duties, specific things that must happen or not happen for the assigned responsibilities to be discharged. In this way the hierarchy creates dependencies. If we don't do what we're supposed to, there's every likelihood that others can't do their things properly. Similarly, if others don't, we can't. It's these responsibilities that enable blame to be apportioned with ease as they're a distinct point of reference in a process or cycle. Responsibility is therefore oriented to what should happen and what did happen. Blame lands in respect of the latter.

Of course, it could be that the fault lies in an intervention external to the expected course of action, but the first thought will always be to trace through the structure. If the salesperson left the factory on time with the product sample on board and didn't arrive at the meeting on time, they're to blame. Traffic?

Diversions? Malfunction? In the mind of the blamed they're relevant circumstances that mitigate or remove fault; in the mind of the blamer, they're just pretexts.

Most blame occurs at a low hum, under the breath. Not grandiose *"J'accuse!"* proclamations for all to hear. Grumbles, passing comments lost on the air we disperse as we move, feelings masked in sarcasm that erode and corrode. As witnesses to the disbursement of blame, we often check ourselves, knowing if we "doth protest too much" we could be next. Thus, do the wheels turn.

While hierarchy intrinsically enables and routes blame, it isn't at fault by default. Hierarchy doesn't have to be rigid. Decision-making and responsibility can be delegated or pushed to those closest to where the customer or key interface resides, to be able to exercise judgment with the benefit of local knowledge and context. In this manner it both mitigates against errors that might attract blame, and where they do occur offers meaningful and accessible context. Hierarchy also allows for specific points within the structure to be replaced and while doing so for the remainder of the system to maintain its cohesion and continue to function as intended. We're less cogs in a machine than joints in an edifice. Responsibility gets re-routed for the duration. There's rarely a clean break in the vertical lines that sustain it. The faster and easier the route to understanding what has gone wrong and why, the less likely blame is to enjoy the time and space to wreak havoc.

What hierarchy cannot do of itself, however, is determine at which point responsibility begins and ends. It can't distinguish between enabling and direct acts or omissions. Enabling may also be conscious or unconscious. It's also unable to determine at which point responsibility ultimately lies. Logically, it should pass directly to the top each time, however minor the matter, as a hierarchy has no breaks in its reporting lines. But, of course, it rarely does given that the lines become greasier the more they connect those with most to lose from such a burden. Firing executives is expensive, disruptive and a PR car crash, after all. At which point the system often relies on standards of decency to continue to function, should any remain. Where responsibility can't be directly attributed in a hierarchy, even if represented by the simple raising of a hand, its credibility evaporates leaving only the exercise of raw power to resolve it.

As humans we're naturally unreliable. We have to try extremely hard not to be. We design processes and deploy equipment and technology to remove the possibility for errors. Yet we're also highly suspicious of automation. As we mentioned car crashes above, take autonomous vehicles. A single accident during testing is decried, but we tolerate poor driving and judgment leading to fatalities every day – according to the WHO, 1.35 million every year.[32] In most such instances, however, it's a question of how long until the technology arrives, not whether.

In some industries, errors simply can't be tolerated, such as hospitals, nuclear facilities, traffic control and submarines. Many have reinvented themselves to become "High Reliability Organizations" (HROs)[33] in which a predisposition to complexity of structure and process ensures the unthinkable is highly unlikely to happen. They're a systemic response to human fragility, the time and investment required for which is vast yet entirely necessary. We wouldn't want to think of them any other way. Imagine living next to a "reasonably reliable" power plant.

The notion of a "no blame" culture has been mooted for those industries not teetering daily on the brink of catastrophe. Why they remain a separate genre of beast is the puzzle at the heart of the workplace fuckery we're trying to dismantle. Investors in People in the UK[34] (once a non-departmental public body, now a "Community Interest Company") identify several features of such organizations, stopping short of suggesting how they might live with the void. They even quaintly ask if such a culture is "right for you." Why on earth it wouldn't be is beyond contemplation. For many who deem it not to be, their slogan might just be: "We're proud to be a chuck-you-under-the-bus outfit. Resilience training is available." But like most beneficial characteristics of organizations that make work an altogether better experience, they involve the body corporate collectively getting off its inherently reluctant arse.

Alternative structures

Hierarchy hasn't had it all its own way. Self-organization, or as it's often called, "spontaneous order," is nothing new. It pre-supposes that imposed or coercive organization is unnecessary and that humans will naturally structure their social and productive relations without the need for direction. Anti-state views were evident in Ancient China through the thinking of Zhuang Zhou in the fourth century BCE, in rejecting authoritarian Confucianism (but all those natty quotes…). The Mazdaks of Persia in the fifth century even managed to convert a king, Kavad I, before thousands of their number were buried headfirst leaving only their feet above the soil to resemble a "human garden." Established authority has always taken this thinking badly.

The philosopher to give the defining political incarnation of self-organization, anarchism, its essential character was Pierre-Joseph Proudhon (1809–1865), he of "all property is theft" repute, heralding a tradition that outflanked Marxism in its belief in the innate human propensity to love and care for one another. Modern interpretations have focused on practical examples, such as the British anarchist Colin Ward in Anarchy in Action.[35] He cites the free and autonomous pre-Welfare State "friendly societies" in the UK as models of self-organization, in which working-class communities collectively organized the provision of local services. Over 200 still operate today. He also highlights services such as the world's post, which without any transfer agreements ensures that letters stamped in one country will be delivered in another. Eventually. Of course, we now have the internet as evidence, together with many of its freely organized networks and offshoots, one of which indirectly gave rise to this book.

We've seen alternatives to hierarchy in corporate life. Some are tweaks to the existing way of things, some are entire revisions. The tweaks include a raft of seemingly nifty diagrammatic representations that effectively default to a modified form of hierarchy. The most prevalent is a networked model, where linear connections appear web-like rather than gravitational, but even the stiffest hierarchy tolerates the development of informal relationships and allows a degree of influence to erode the formality of instruction. Hierarchy also encourages peer groups to form at common levels within organizations. "Tribe" models borrow the language of Agile software development in creating a second, overlaid organizational model based around project or customer teams involving people from a variety of formal departments. We each reside in both. They necessitate a whole raft of tools and processes with juvenile names that cry out for silly hats, somewhat undermining the seriousness of their intent.

An organizational approach without the sniggering is created with a "circle" structure, where multidisciplinary teams congregate around sub-sets of the organization's overall purpose. This has found form in something genuinely different. "Holacracy," given substance by Brian Robertson at Ternary Software in 2007[36], distributes authority through a "holarchy" of self-organizing teams or "holons[37]," a Greek word first used in this context by Arthur Koestler in 1967[38], in which each is both a whole and a part. Koestler described this form as "self-organizing holarchic open systems" – or, conveniently, SOHO. Which is cool with a lot of effort.

While holacracy still retains a degree of authority and

structure, we're closer in the corporate world than with the other pretenders to something Colin Ward may have recognized. It surgically removes the ability for blame to be identified and to flow, instead allowing issues to be resolved within circles that have the inherent propensity to be rationally, emotionally and physically safe. It's an idea that warrants wider experimentation.

The desire for personal autonomy was identified by Daniel Pink in his much-traveled 2009 book *Drive*.[39] He maintains that the control of what we do, when we do it and who we do it with provides our necessary motivation to get up in the morning. We just need to add mastery (the ability to do it) and purpose (a good reason why we do it) for "Motivation 3.0," improving on 1.0 (mere survival) and 2.0 (carrot and stick), while recognizing that many organizations are still stuck with the reward and punishment model. Some with survival. On this basis self-organization becomes the free association of self-directed individuals: we know it makes sense and decide, unconstrained, to do it. Mastery and purpose might indeed be motivators for anyone in any occupation, but as we identified in the previous chapter, with control there's an air of privilege attached that would only be recognizable to the knowledge worker or artisan. Interestingly, too, Pink responded in an interview that the three drives were a possible "reflection of the things he values most, and not necessarily an objective view on reality."[40]

We shouldn't forget that with freedom, as positioned by Pink and as holacracy offers, comes responsibility. We like to talk about freedom at work, demand it even. But responsibility is a bit trickier. Clear and rigid hierarchy offers a convenience. We talk about decisions being at a "pay grade." We're happy to be a joint. From our lowlier position we can assign responsibility one stage higher and have someone more senior instruct us what to do. We may make it easier and illustrate our diligence by presenting options. When instruction is received, we sometimes obtain or confirm it in writing so we can stuff it down the back of our tunic. Just in case. It can feel like a game of pass-the-parcel we don't want to win.

Whose fault is blame?

On the face of it, any mention of blame may immediately imply something entirely crap in the receiving, giving or merely witnessing. That might be enough. On evaluation, it reveals itself to be even more so than we might initially imagine.

First, more than anything, it's demeaning. Time freezes in that moment before impact, when we know we've goofed and the crunching of metal and shattering of glass is inevitable. When we're aware, we don't need to be told. We know. But someone insists on telling us because their role necessitates it. As suggested at the outset, we agonize over whether to accept or deflect, or perhaps some of each – I did x, but I didn't expect y too. Somehow acknowledging a degree of culpability plays the hierarchy at its own game, throwing its need for certainty into confusion. Yet others form their judgment, causing blame to work on two levels – that which is ascribed and that which becomes story. Even legend. They're often distant, but they're both ours. The resulting anxiety has a long tail, adding to that considered in Chapter 3. In both instances we hope that a combination of time and a chance to do something more noticeably positive will eradicate it. All the while we're living with it. And hating it.

Second, even on enquiry, establishing the ultimate extent of responsibility in a situation is often random and inconsistent, so blame will only ever be far more so. Blame precedes the establishment of fault, it's instant, innocence needs to be proven. Fault is established thereafter to justify the blame having been apportioned or prompting the blame to be shifted. There's no universal guide, and every situation is unique. "Blame and how to land it first time, every time" isn't a chapter in the staff handbook. In simple instances, the attribution is to the person directly responsible for what should have (or not) happened. In some it's their manager, whether they were even aware of what was happening, as it's deemed they should have been – which runs counter to the encouragement to trust and delegate. Yet complexity often obscures the path, the knowledge and its timing. It can be a single event or a trend. It's safe to say that but for the most straightforward of situations, blame will always appear arbitrary to all involved, heightening the sense of unfairness. Blame comes with injustice as standard.

Third, it's mired in mixed messages. We're told it's good to fail because we're trying stuff. We're even asked to "fail fast" – cock it up quickly. When we experiment, some things work, some don't. Failure, historically an ultimately negative outcome, is flipped into a positive. We've vitally closed off an avenue. Napoleon probably learned a lot of useful stuff from his attempt to conquer Russia, and we can be sure they had a damn good wash-up at the whiteboard when the remnants of his army got back to Paris. The statement: "The most exciting phrase to hear in science, the one that heralds new discoveries, is not 'Eureka!' (I found it!) but 'That's funny...'" has been attributed on a thousand motivational posters to Isaac Asimov but was probably down to Alexander Fleming.[41] It suggests that often what we're working on reveals something else entirely. Like the parade of proud experienced by those in clinical trials of a cardiovascular drug in the early 1990s, the Y-front buster that became the commercial blockbuster, Viagra.[42] More interesting than sticky notes. It ended up being used for its original intended purpose later, too, as the yielding of alternative results through scientific experimentation leading to multiple uses is fairly normal.

But unless we're in a laboratory where the entire purpose of our existence and the standard on which we're evaluated is discovery, the rules and expectations are entirely different. Failure isn't as glamorous as the scatty, white-coated rock stars of innovation or the sticky-note plonking (the invention was especially useful for them) facilitators of transformation suggest. The luxury of spending time trying new stuff *just in case* is rarely afforded the corporate foot soldier, expected as they are to simply get things right and not waste any time or money. Least of all is "failing fast" welcome on a production line. In a hierarchical structure, failure needs to be specifically attributed. Even if it's a failure from which we learn and something good results. Consequently, blame kills innovation. For all the negative human impact that a shamelessly merciless executive might shrug off as cultural shrapnel, there's a bottom-line consequence. The irony.

Fourth, blame is often disproportionate in its reach and lifespan. It's like a limpet mine: always there, threatening to blow. There's almost no amount of excellence that can erase the story, it simply exists alongside it. "Samantha, yes, she sold the ten biggest contracts of the year but totally messed up the partnership deal. *What* a hairball that was. She's not going anywhere." As we'll discover there's an overt and sinister inequality bias to blame too. Some members of the workforce are expected, due to the prejudices of their colleagues, to be more likely to screw up, or to have the scale of their screw up magnified. The volume and drone depend on the blame chorus. Not the one blaming, but the others in near shot who, in an attempt to win favor or place themselves on their chosen side of history, repeat it. They can stop. They can move on, let it be forgotten. If there are no other stories to tell we usually continue to tell the same ones over and over. The onus is on us all to refuse to take part, not to listen and certainly not to repeat. We may not have the courage to front it out with the perpetrator, for any number of reasons, but we certainly don't have to feed it.

Fifth, because there's no evidence required, blame can be a defensive tactic of the guilty or an offensive tool of the unscrupulous. For the practitioner, it's a case of "speed to market." The faster and louder blame can be leveled at someone clearly not at fault, the more time is created to ensure the evidence can be removed or obscured before the truth is revealed. Fortunately, haste and volume are the dead giveaways. In a similar vein it can also be used in the pursuit of a personal agenda or ambition, more likely at an ambient level. Blame is a political weapon. The subtle, anonymous planting of the seedling of a story in the vicinity of undiscerning voices can be enough, with a little watering, to derail the momentum of another as they're required to defend their position. All without confrontation or the revealing of a hand. Such instances are much harder to detect until a pattern emerges.

Finally, apportioning blame is a core characteristic of bullying. Along with – and often alongside or fired by – the prejudice to which we referred and shall refer again, in behavioral terms this is probably the very worst experience the workplace presents. One person's misguided idea of clear no-nonsense direction issued to a supposedly under-performing subordinate is another's blatant maltreatment. As such it's incredibly difficult to identify and prove, with no clear cut, objective characteristics. It's not always consistent such that we can see it coming. To a large degree its effect is dependent on the resilience or emotional state of the bullied. Yet it's invariably corrosive to the mental health of the recipient, to the point where it can impact physical health. At its extreme, for some, even the mortal coil proves too much to bear at the prospect of its continuance.

Coming forward to report bullying takes significant courage. Doubt as a junior party of being believed and understood often delays the situation surfacing, on too many occasions even at all. The necessary evidence requires credible witnesses prepared to speak, themselves fearful of the consequences, or the use of devious methods. Raising the matter can even be interpreted to be mischievous or vindictive, meeting a collective denial that turns the victim into the perpetrator. Whistle-blower schemes can help, until reckless or frightened executives publicly announce the hunt for those daring to take comfort from the promised anonymity. Often the recipient simply slips away silently, shattered, broken, the fearful observers glad it wasn't them this time and hoping it won't be them the next.

Bullies are often masters of their depressing trade, covering their tracks with fresh soil or stellar performance. They make themselves too valuable to fire, their results justifying their methods. Questionable behavior is brushed away as just "them being them." As with the vocal blamers, they're often the loudest protestors of poor behavior in others, creating a smokescreen of decency. Where they're identified and the organization has no choice but to act, it often does so softly. Bullying is bad publicity, not simply relating to the incident itself but because the conclusion often drawn is that it's widespread, part of the organizational fabric. Bullies beget bullies. A bullying culture is a blame culture. A swift and beefily bunced compromise agreement and a quiet exit to "pursue other opportunities" later and the ripples harmlessly reach the bank, their energy dissipated. Until the next time.

Un-f✱cking responsibility

No-one but the sadist sets out with a specific intent to create a blame culture. Which means some do. Invariably, it emerges and breeds where there's an over-emphasis on personal responsibility in what is an innately collective endeavor. Its incremental solidification is barely noticeable from within. The realization it's present can generate a desire to respond quickly and firmly, to shatter it, toe-to-toe, at a distinctly human level. Like we once had to in the school playground, when we could finally take no more, knowing it would probably hurt but would be worth it when healed. But it's a systemic solution we're after.

The balance between personal and collective responsibility is delicate but achievable. We all contribute to the collective, we have a part to play. Others are reliant on us, we on them. Where we cause something to go wrong, the collective may suffer. But as the simple summation of the individual doesn't equal the collective, it's subordinate to it in each case. The negative effect on the collective from an individual error can be alleviated by others within where there's unconditional care for one another. The learning can be shared and understood. Practices can change if deemed deficient. Blame is eradicated when it's starved of oxygen, when it serves no purpose.

Our statement, reflecting the essential need for this balance, therefore becomes:

"~~It's not a blame culture~~"

"We're all responsible – to ourselves and one another"

It's a positive statement, not a denial of something negative. Responsibility isn't blame in softer shoes. It's an active, organic creator of relationships. Which means it's not just a list of things expected to function or occur (or not, depending on how it's framed) on our watch; it defines how we and others relate and operate. What we do makes what others do possible. We're not alone, and no-one deserves to be made to feel that way.

We might choose three paths to unraveling the claustrophobia of a blame culture.

First, it's doubtless that non-hierarchical approaches to organization reduce the potential for blame to persist. They remove the linear transfer of power and control on which it thrives, instead centering small groups around common purpose. Blame can no longer run the grid; it remains within the circles in which it might have surfaced and can be resolved together. While personal autonomy resonates with us all, we also need to remember that the organization is a community, and we need to think and act in its service. Self-organization can't flourish without an overriding community mindset. While some have maintained that such a view settles out of its own accord, organizations may not have the luxury of the time to allow it to form naturally. Competing agendas slow and stymie the process. Our freedom must be shared within a model that works for us all.

We might consider that such a radical structural transformation is beyond the wit, patience or competence of our organization; that other priorities will always take precedence over resolving isolated cases of personal injustice. There may also be a perceived risk of disproportionate negative consequences elsewhere. But there will be opportunities too. Such a proposition will always be a test of resolve. How much do we want to fix this crap?

We must also consider how blame can be eradicated irrespective of the structure in which we operate. It begins with us, our own self-awareness and desire to improve. We shouldn't have to design better systems to try and force us to be better humans – as has been the tendency – as in doing so we abdicate responsibility; we're not invested in their success. We should become better humans such that we can design and develop better systems. Priorities will change and we'll evolve those systems, but the systems will change us too. As Heraclitus, the Ancient Greek philosopher of change noted, we never step twice in the same river – both the river and we have moved on.

Second, therefore, we must replace blame with understanding. In this way that essential component of organizational life, responsibility, flourishes. We can thrive on it, even when daunted or scared by it. It can be the motivator it's purported to be and set us free. The complexity of most events requires us to understand as far as possible where human and systemic responsibility lies such that we can ensure the negative doesn't happen or happen again. It will invariably be a combination of both. And with the human aspect, rarely just one of our number. Obtaining understanding can't take the inquisitorial, root canal approach associated with "fault-finding" as this will yield little that can be trusted. If we seek it in such a way that it prompts honesty, we'll get honesty. Honesty is beautifully infectious. Just as blame is grotesquely so. It's up to us which we choose.

Finally, we raise the hand. Without pausing to weigh up the risk. If we feel the system is fair, if we know the goal is understanding, we'll be content to do so. Those who see this happening will follow the lead, we grant that permission irrespective of where our joint in the grid resides. We should be under no illusion, however; it's not a free pass to incompetence. It doesn't absolve us from responsibility. But it makes sure no-one else is wrongly deemed the cause. Sometimes we're happy to step forward to "take one for the team" because we're in a place where it's possible or necessary, or we see the consequences as minimal. We may just wish to move on. That's a matter for us. If we lead a team, when it goes well, we step aside and promote their contribution, when it goes badly, we visibly accept responsibility. Because that's the kind of team we'd love to be working in. It all returns, in one way or another, to our behaving in the way we'd like to be treated.

Chapter 5

"We trust our people"

But we don't. Do we?

Tossing up whether a ruler should be loved or feared, Niccolò Machiavelli opted for the latter in his most famous tract, *The Prince* (1513).[43] He was, of course, at the time shamelessly sucking up to Lorenzo de Medici, the ruler of Florence, in the hope of favor. He had just been forced to leave the kingdom as a political exile, after all. Having studied the dubious methods of Cesare Borgia (1475-1507) he backed the option that looked most promising, holding that the dominance of our own interests would always result in us needing the hearty and credible threat of a beating to comply with direction. Trust didn't come into it if fear was available and deliverable. His work became the operating manual of every unprincipled power-intoxicated shyster thereafter and still resonates with bespoke-tailored autocratic wannabes half a millennium later.

We've been saddled with the idea of realpolitik ever since, even though the actual term wasn't coined by journalist Ludwig von Rochau until 1853. Sun Tzu, beloved guru of the boardroom book club, was plowing this groove long before even Machiavelli. Practical, pragmatic, opportunistic. How it is rather than how we think or believe it should be or want or strive for it to be. By this mantra, we're lumbered with the fact that humans are fundamentally devious where power is at stake – and that power is always at stake. There's a sense too in this idea that there can never be enough power. History is awash with examples of demagogues who've risen within a supportive nucleus only at the appropriate time to violently peel it away, creating a safe distance from anyone with similar designs. There are many of them with us today, some in surprising places. Of course, in thought and practice it's been an almost entirely privileged male domain. Given its tradition, that we can now recognize and call it out as such constitutes progress, if not far too little.

As with many of the ideas in this book, realpolitik ports itself into the innately political modern workplace, re-sizing and re-shaping to fit. Therein, trust is possibly the most over-promised, over-promoted, under-delivered and evident workplace idea – as something we can identify and seek – of them all. And it's a crowded field. Just about everyone agrees that trust matters and it's important. No-one's going to tell us it's irrelevant. Not to our face, at any rate. So, we could be forgiven for thinking that it's on every breath, flourishing between the slabs of MDF, crackling across the Wi-Fi, lubricating our every interaction. But it's not. At least not in the ways we imagine it should.

Because even Niccolò failed to acknowledge that trust underpins every aspect of human existence. Society *is* trust. It's people doing what they say they're going to do. Confucius was onto this when he said, "I wouldn't know what to do with someone whose word cannot be trusted. How would you drive a wagon without a yoke or a chariot without a crossbar?[44]" Far from the Hobbesian nightmare of a life that's "solitary, poor, nasty, brutish and short[45]," conceived in the days when philosophers would imagine what it was all like before their wisdom was gifted upon a world that didn't realize it was needed.

Even the most primitive of societies had trust. A "war of all against all" as Hobbes would have it would mean nothing ever got made, built or operated, as we'd be pre-occupied with fighting everyone else – rather like the chaotic English Civil Wars that provided the fearful context for his famous work, *Leviathan* (1651), from which these quotes are taken. Humanity would have all been over rather quickly.

It explains our horror when events appear to slip through a tear in the fabric of reality and someone does something randomly horrific. Mass shootings, common in countries where the instruments of death are readily available, but not unknown in others too, are a modern example. Investigation usually exposes seething resentment, mental vulnerability or indoctrination. Or all the above. Motive, however remote from our understanding, emerges.

Like an iceberg, below the waterline there's the everyday, fundamental and unconscious trust that just is, that ensures society functions and we don't all arbitrarily butcher one another; and that which protrudes and which is evident, conscious and negotiable. We're dealing in the workplace with the latter.

Trust is a simple idea, and remarkably simple to practice. We just have to want to. At its heart, it helps us all get stuff done, confident that there'll be no negative repercussions. We can trust someone (use it), show we trust someone (gift it) and accept it being gifted to us (take it). Each of which can be conscious or unconscious, rationalized or instinctive. It's catchy too. Ernest Hemingway, in a private letter, once wrote: "The way to make people trust-worthy is to trust them.[46]" It doesn't get simpler than that. Mistrust is equally viral. Only trust is difficult to build and easy to destroy, while mistrust is easy to build and monstrous to repair.

Doubt

Somewhere in the no-person's land between the two is doubt, a form of relationship purgatory common in the workplace, where we're thrown together with people we're told – or often it's merely implied – are "on the same side." Supposedly offered as a comfort, it can more often than not feel like a warning. At least facing those not on our side, wearing different colors, we can be justified in our doubt. But we're never entirely sure. Even, ridiculously, with those people we've had a say in bringing into the team or with those that have brought us in, where validation by others has been sought, where eyes have met, and we've had a peek through to the soul. Our success or failure therefore hangs by its gossamer thread. We're cautious, hesitant, non-committal. We blotch caveats into every crevice in our interactions. We leave doors ajar, escape routes from our assurances, as we see them similarly left by those with whom we interact. In our in-between state the best we can offer or be offered is the benefit of the doubt. This implies trust can be used selectively, deployed, weaponized. It's unsettling, while also being strangely comforting, to know that "yes" always translates as "possibly." Even the language of trust is innately diluted daily.

Beyond the security barriers, we're dealing with the tiny sliver of trust that makes all the difference. We can't possibly be who we think we are. We haven't done what we said we have. We can't do what we say we can do. We can't want what we say we want. It'll only be believed when it's seen. And even when seen it may not be believed. That it happens to us, and we resent being made to feel this way, we respond in the natural manner. We perpetuate it. We don't believe we deserve to feel crap alone. The fundamental difficulty with overt displays of trust is that it's tough to gift them when all around are refusing to do likewise. We offer ourselves up for exploitation. Best, therefore, not to, just in case.

And so, we get to the idea that trust at work has to be earned. While the involuntary societal interactions between us are accepted, for everything else we begin with an empty slate. There are no universal rules or norms about how much we must do to earn trust, or what form it takes. A minor beneficial act – like an unexpected latte? A month of affirmation? Taking one for the team where the consequences are notable but unlikely to be lasting? Fishing them from a frozen pond into which they recklessly dived to save their cockapoo on a mid-February afternoon? No, it's a matter of the arbitrary judgment of the beholder. Similarly, we're never entirely sure when what has been earned might be spent. The pneumonia may have been for nothing after failing to agree with an unworkable suggestion made in a meeting no-one wanted to be at.

Trust is often the missing ingredient in workplace myth. Take the moments of serendipity where, adjacent to an item of office detritus, we achieve the ultimate corporate connection, a monetizable idea. In a story told only by content-starved bloggers and first-role workplace designers, we supposedly find common interest and intent in the spark of friction from our accidental encounters. The importance of these "watercooler moments" – forgetting the fact that the device is usually stationed somewhere no-one wants to loiter for any longer than it takes to hydrate – has been massively overplayed. There's precious little evidence that they yield what the myth portrays, because unless trust already exists between the participants, conversations of the type imagined, with their open sharing of insights and ideas, don't happen. That's not to say that such an interaction may not prove to be the first tentative step toward a relationship that later proves fruitful.

Yet the significance of these interactions has similarly been underplayed. They're so often personal exchanges between those where trust already exists. It's because there's trust that confidences can be exchanged, reassurances given, fears put to rest. They're the vital and necessary moments in which we find calm. Not where amazing ideas are born. Yet no-one creates myths about that kind of thing.

Safety

Trust operates at an individual and a group level. It's complex enough at the former, but geometrically problematic at the latter. For 30 years the idea of "psychological safety" has rattled around predominantly American academia, unable to break the shackles of the original moniker gifted by William Kahn.[47] He suggested this was a condition where we can show ourselves without fear of judgment. An open rather than a safe space. It's a vital, non-negotiable and exception-free condition of an un-fucked workplace. It's strange that it needs a term or definition at all, but that's essentially because in most workplaces it's absent. Where it exists, it erodes stress, speeds transactions between us and builds social cohesion. Yet if we can't explain it, if no-one knows enough of its criticality to demand it, if no-one feels as though it can possibly apply to them, if it's kept conveniently caged in a shaded corner of introspection, it's utterly pointless. Perhaps that was always the plan?

The term also omits to include physical safety, the basis of the #MeToo movement that began in 2017 where the threat or actuality of personal harm to women in the workplace prompted a global movement to identify and, where possible, prosecute the perpetrators. It's all very well feeling safe to think or say something, but trust extends to knowing that sexual harassment or attack isn't a likely outcome of our interactions. Or that when it occurs, disbelief that it could have done so – or even blame of the recipient, as the perpetrator becomes the victim – an all-too-likely response, as was evaluated in the previous chapter. The real aim is therefore simply safety. No defining prefix needed, beautifully simple. Without the fundamental condition of safety – to think, feel and act, the total human experience – trust doesn't stand a living chance. It's an absolute pre-requisite.

Mistrust

The barren landscape of trust plays out in several ways beneath the parasol of what has become known as "micromanagement." That is, the close control of the activities of subordinates. It manifests itself in four forms of observation – looking at us directly, looking over our shoulder, looking at everything we create, or looking at us through an application.

Before we summon the specter of managers past who have subjected us to any one or more of these forms of what we often deem humiliation, it's worth considering when we've been the perpetrator. We'll have rationalized it, for sure, because when *we* do stuff there's always a valid reason. Incompetence, urgency, results, or pressure, perhaps. When others do it there isn't and they're just an unmitigated arse. It's the rule of self. The ownness to which we previously referred. Fessing up at this point is cleansing if not hideously embarrassing. But if you leave this paragraph without an admission, you're probably not being entirely honest with yourself.

The practice of a manager surveying workers to ensure that set tasks are completed is as old as work itself. Trust wasn't a management concept in play where livelihoods were at stake daily and margins were fine. In the anonymized corporate world where ownership and labor are separated by ranks and often oceans, it's easy to forget that if *we're* paying someone out of our own pocket to do something, we expect it to be done, and done properly. Assuming, of course, that the complexity of the task, the time allowed, the suitability of the environment, the clarity of the instruction, the materials and resources provided and the supposed competence of the contributor of the service are all deemed appropriate. That's a lot of dependent factors. That's what organizations are supposed to do – ensure that they're met. It takes a lot of people doing a lot of things for that to happen. People do work to make sure other people can do work. If people don't do the work properly to make sure other people can do the work properly, it all flips belly up.

We might call management by observation "panoptic management" after utilitarian all-rounder Jeremy Bentham's supposedly humanitarian prison design of the 1780s, the Panopticon. The design comprised a central control tower with cells arrayed around it, allowing a single guard in the tower to see into the cells but the prisoners not to see the guard. In this manner, not knowing whether they were being watched, the prisoners would always behave as though they were under observation. Savage genius, it's likely to have been acknowledged in some traditional quarters as the optimal workplace design. No-one has been bold enough to openly admit it, naturally.

If not directly surveying those before them, "management by wandering about" (MBWA) provides an opportunity for close-up scrutiny and enquiry. Managers essentially get to spend their time annoying their charges by appearing over their shoulders just as the subject is entering their payment details, all under the auspices of the applied theory of random sampling. Of course, all wandering isn't the same. It can be anything from skulking (I don't want you to know) to purposeful stomping (I sure as heck want you to know).

For office workers, the introduction of the Modern Efficiency Desk in 1915, a flat metal creation that gave the hapless worker nowhere to hide behind handy stacks of papers, and the integral storage units of the Wooton, its homely predecessor, assisted the practice.[48] As did the open plan environments typical of the day which began to re-emerge in the 1960s, making visibility all the easier. Such workplace design was sold as an aid to communication and interaction, as leaders become accessible and approachable, without our thinking they might be close enough to feel their breath on our neck. Some managers can make such random presence work effectively, offering guidance and mentoring as they go, but it's likely they would make any environment work.

We may have been forgiven for thinking that the idea of "handing our work in" might have been left at the school gates on our final exit, but the request for output to be submitted in draft, or to be "run by" a manager persists as a monitoring technique, particularly where manager and charge aren't in the same location. Even when dressed in the finery of awareness, responsibility, quality control or even development. As will be explored below, at times one we're happy to comply with.

The difficulty in an age where a considerable amount of work takes place through a screen, even in non-office locations, is to establish whether anyone's actually doing anything useful at all. A determined expression can mask hours of irresponsible yet ultimately satisfying piddling around. Visual supervision became able to identify only whether someone was present. Output could be periodically checked, but that took no account of speed and effectiveness. The higher caliber the operative, the more time became available for amusement. It's a wonder no-one thought to put the individual in charge at the other end of the workplace so everyone had their back to them, with screens facing. Born of this managerial frustration, technological applications have been developed to place the eyes on the inside, the tachographs of the digital age. MBWA amid circuits and wires.

This book was written during one of several UK lockdowns as a result of the global Covid-19 pandemic. Trust became a focal point as the first enforced absence from Gormenghast fractured presence-dependent management structures, leaving many responsible folk feeling helplessly devoid of control. It was a beautiful moment. After some weeks of a distributed-work necessity for many, once deemed unfeasible and undesirable, skeptics of the arrangement quietly began to admit it wasn't so bad, as a uniquely personal bond with their jogging pants and slippers was formed. All that was missing was that vital management tool of old: visibility.

Ultimately nothing says "I trust you" like a keystroke monitor installed on our laptop. Or screen grabs, or desk chair cushion sensors, or wrist bands. There's an all-inclusive suite in reflection reserved for the originators of software to track personal performance in this manner, adjacent to that for all those who request them. It's kit created because it's possible, not because it's the right thing to do. It comes with assurances to calm the nerves of the understandably uncomfortable. That they're supposedly consensual masks that such agreement from the observed is often conditional on remaining in the job. That they're purely for identifying process improvement opportunities ignores the temptation for unscrupulous use. They can pinpoint fault for the precision-targeted application of once-daubed blame. Within the catch-all for the malicious and sinister resuscitation of practices dating back millennia, "people analytics," organizations have been gifted near-perfect Taylorism lurking beneath the mystique of chirpy start-ups with snappy, jovial names. For the proponents, it's another bug-ridden ventilation shaft to the executive suite. At the expense not just of everyone else, but ultimately themselves too.

The Covid era saw an initial knee-jerk and entirely misplaced celebration of the return of management by output. As in, individually quantified productivity. Of course, the celebrants were in pursuit of "likes" mistaking their accumulation for credibility. What became apparent over time, with a little prompting, was that – as we established in Chapter 2 – outside of manufacturing, extraction and logistics, much of what work comprises isn't output, it's contribution. The gift economy in full bloom, particularly for many given the need to bridge the isolation from working under house arrest. In such an environment, the cameras and counters and stokers of the ether in the hands of the people analyzers have proven perplexed. Their focus on the algorithmically straightforward realm of quantity means they fail in regard to measuring quality. They also can't detect whether they're measuring different people doing the same thing. Just because they're measuring something doesn't mean to say it's useful or meaningful. We'll get to measurement in Chapter 10.

We can't forget that we've been complicit in the methods of physical observation in two respects – to gain credit and avoid blame.

That we supposedly perform better when we know we're being observed has become known as the "Hawthorne effect" from the 1920s productivity experiments in the USA. Taking this a step further, knowing that we're being watched has proven to be a path to recognition, favor or promotion if it's deemed we're doing something well. When it works, we make ourselves and our work more visible. It's the equivalent of scrolling, only played out in slow motion; the dopamine search, the hope of greater rewards to come. So, we encourage observation by placing ourselves in its path and seeking the cues that we've been clocked. How reassuring for a manager to find that with every sweeping glance across the workplace that their people are steering themselves into their line of sight with the visual evidence of their presence, commitment and creations. We've unknowingly been validating and perpetuating it. Of course, that all gets rather complicated when it comes to digital surveillance. The game loses its human character, and our ability to optimize the opportunities the system presents diminishes, such that for those who mastered the ancient art, the playing field seems unfairly flat. We just have to bash out those keystrokes or place a large weight on our chair like everyone else.

Our participation is also helpful where we'd rather not be undertaking a task or creating what's required. It may be unpopular, unpleasant, even incendiary. In which case better we've had it reviewed and even edited from above. Sometimes we offer that which we've created even when not requested, seeking the inherent protection of the organizational structure. Hierarchy can be useful.

The post-Covid world of office work is set to be characterized by "hybrid" approaches, with physical presence in the workplace balanced with time spent locally – in another of the organization's buildings or a flexible space of some form – or, in all probability, at home. They've been exquisitely described as "the bastard offspring of flexible working and shift work.[49]" The relative success of the year of remote working has proven that digital tools are adequate for many tasks. Yet this presents a further visibility challenge associated with "mixed mode" patterns of attendance – a formally dressed version of "fear of missing out" (FoMo), the sense that those present are far more likely to be in leaders' eyelines and hence thoughts when it comes to involvement, rewards and promotion. This form of proximity bias has yet, at the time of writing, to be proven at scale, but it's lurking. And we know it's there. For all non-office workers, nothing in this regard has changed. The reassuring analog methods are still very much in play.

Of course, wherever we are, work needs to be done and done well. And a contribution needs to be made. So how do we ensure that it happens, that communication is open, two-way and honest, that both managers and their teams are available when they need to be and are trusted to do what they say they will do? There will always be those who commit more and those who commit less. Some who don't commit at all. How do we un-fuck it for everyone's benefit?

Un-f*cking trust

The organization is its people. The two aren't distinct. For an organization to say it trusts its people makes no logical sense. Even if we surmise that it should read that an organization's senior management trust their people, they have to be trusted and trust one another too. And where do we draw the line at "senior?" It's also the case that trust thrives or dies; it's not static, frozen interaction. It needs to be nurtured and demonstrated. Our statement therefore becomes:

"~~We trust our people~~"

"We build trust"

In this sense we're giving trust energy, life. We're making clear an intent, in striving toward which it becomes dynamic. It's never finished. If we think it is, *we're* finished.

A more mutually supportive future may be secured in three ways.

First, we make trust a condition of belonging. Not an optional extra available only in deluxe roles, a matter of judgment, personal preference, or any degree of relativity. It's so often regarded as simply something we should inherently understand, promote and practice. It's assumed that life has taught us its value and the methods of enhancing it, but through experience and observation of the questionable ways of others it may well have schooled us in the opposite. Even if we still say all the right things at interview. Trust isn't up to us, it simply *has to be*. There can be no reliance on the organization's position on trust being painted on the wall, embedded in an intranet site, or hidden in a statement of values that no-one can quite locate or is due for review. It must be made clear at the very outset, at the beginning of the relationship. It can't be something that has to be earned, because we have to work together from the very outset. From there, it can be built.

Second, we dismantle the personal agendas that drive mistrust. Those same agendas that can prompt the application of blame in their service. We establish collective goal setting and evaluation, we share accountability and the criteria for success, and we make each known to everyone. Where any sense of unfairness is detected, it's addressed openly and never goes unresolved. It means making tough calls. That's very often what we're there for. In doing so we de-construct the secrecy in all its guises inherent within any organization. Trust thrives on openness and transparency, even when it's awkward or difficult. The reverse is therefore true. Walls, doors and locks may be the physical manifestation of a "need-to-know" *modus operandi*, but the intangible barriers are more menacing. From the manner in which conversations occur, information is distributed and handled, and concerns are raised and addressed. None are left to ferment.

We should remember too that when we were all present in the workplace for the majority of the time, we would often see who was talking to who, even if we didn't hear what was being said. Glass-fronted rooms offered little protection. In a more distributed environment, as will be the case for many, where conversations happen online, we have no idea. The imperative for transparency has been magnified.

Trust is oxygen, its supply cannot be blocked. Third, therefore, is continual awareness. What it means, why it's important, how to deal with situations where it's broken down, and how to create the path back. That means sharing positive stories where trust played a vital role. Its absence is called out openly, at the time of it being identified, the reasons established, the return to trust established. All of this within an environment of non-negotiable, complete and assured safety – rational, emotional and physical. For trust and safety are inseparable. We can't have a viable, functioning workplace without both.

While it's everyone's imperative, a beneficial grounding in trust can prepare managers for any challenge, including distributed working and variable workplace attendance. Trust is, after all, location-agnostic. In this way we also dilute and eventually eradicate the perceived need for intrusive approaches and technologies that are diminishing to the observed and monitored. Naturally, there will be difficult situations to handle, some requiring remedial measures. Yet in such instances, if everyone can say with a clear conscience that it was handled fairly, we'll be succeeding. Present tense. It's never over.

As a final thought. With blame, we strive to see it vanish from our lives entirely. We don't wish to experience it; we don't wish to witness it. We're not in pursuit of its opposite, as such – we just don't want it, as it serves no objectively beneficial purpose.

Yet we crave trust in order to banish its opposite, mistrust. Ultimately, we can't obscure the fact that irrespective of what we do or where in the organization we do it, the feeling of being trusted is exhilarating. Our chest expands and we breathe deeper, our stride lengthens. We're confident, we're patient, we listen, we're aware. It's a physiological as well as an emotional response.

Who wouldn't want that?

Chapter 6

"We're an equal opportunities employer"

But we're not, are we?

The phrase has two parts – equality and opportunity. The focus here will primarily be on the former, as this presents the deepest challenge and one that's both societal and organizational. We walk inequality from the streets through the revolving door.

Practically, equality is entirely possible. In 2010 the Equality Act was passed in the UK with the purpose of eliminating discrimination, promoting equality and fostering good relations in respect of every possible aspect of who we are and how we choose to be. There are no specific limiting factors of which we know that would prevent the Act being implemented in full in every organization across each of its nine protected characteristics: age, disability, gender reassignment, marriage and civil partnership, pregnancy and maternity, race, religion or belief, sex and sexual orientation.

The Act has beneficially (in principle at least) served to create positions within many organizations responsible for diversity – the fact – and the resulting choices they may make relating to equality and inclusion. For some, there was already such a role. For others it's simply meant appointing someone from a disadvantaged minority, for others appointing someone from a disadvantaged minority and then preventing them getting anything done. There's a long way to go before it's considered anything other than niche; but a start worthy of recognition, nonetheless.

The issue to date has been that the good intention has been subject to the influence of societally necessary movements such as #MeToo (2018) and #BlackLivesMatter (2020). They've diverted attention into intense yet narrow channels rather than ensuring irreversible advance is made across the entire breadth of inequality. At the time of writing, race discrimination remains the dominant focus and has become a battleground in what have become known as "culture wars," where polarized social groups struggle for the dominance of their values and practices.[50]

We also have to recognize that there are glaring omissions from the nine characteristics, not least neurodiversity. When up to one in seven of the working population are deemed to be neurodivergent, in that their cognitive functions are at odds with systems, processes and spaces created by organizations for neurotypical colleagues, the challenge takes on an even more complex hue. That neurodiversity has a strong correlation with creativity means that many organizations are disadvantaging not just many of their people, but themselves.

If we were to attempt to cover all nine characteristics – and those missing, yet equally worthy of consideration – in one short essay, we'd be skidding over pack ice. So, we'll consider equal opportunities through the lens of that protection affecting the largest number – gender. Respecting the many nuances of the subject, we'll do so in terms of simply male and female. Even in this area there's a lot to consider, such that it's like trying to fit an ocean into a test tube. And so many others – like Linda Scott[51] and Caroline Criado Perez[52] and Mary Beard[53] and many more – have said it so much better.

Before we consider opportunities in terms of our comparatively cosseted careers in the "developed" world, we sometimes forget that in many countries women have no rights or protection at all: to their status, assets or even their own physical being. Their struggle is fundamental, but we're barely aware of their exposure to almost primitive societal norms and the havoc and pain they wreak. Women have no recourse when wronged, no appeal when accused. They're merely a commodity for men to do with as they please without consequence. The Covid-19 pandemic has in many locations created "disaster patriarchy," where the dreadful plight of women has been hugely exacerbated.[54] That's not to deny that religion and race, among other characteristics, have left a bloodstained trail through history, and continue to fuel conflict today. Yet in many countries the women subject to this barbarity are the majority. This explains our focus. By rights, there should be no-one left in a developed economy who isn't a feminist.

In cities of paved streets and personal space, there's much talk in the pursuit of equality of the idea of "unconscious bias." That is, making unfair judgments based on a subtle trigger of which we're not specifically aware. Like hearing a name and drawing an immediate conclusion from our pre-loaded prejudice. There are at least a dozen types.[55] While it's absolutely "a thing," we appear to have moved to the unconscious before solving the more evident conscious bias. The stuff that's right in our face. When we understand from credible studies that both women and men are twice as likely to select a male candidate for a role over a woman, or that women in the UK have been disproportionately affected by redundancy during the Covid-19 pandemic (17 percent made redundant compared to 4 percent of men)[56] we begin to realize that the "unconscious" aspect is a convenient smokescreen for entirely conscious choices. It makes it appear as though without highly specialist guidance we're helpless to dark forces in our psyche, when we could instead decide to stop being an arse.

The issue is: to be an equal opportunities employer, we first have to *want* to be. Then, we must stop making excuses, and just bloody well get on with it.

Biology

We can trace the issues faced by women in the workplace through points in a lifespan. We begin with the tricky subject of biology. In terms of the big issues, there are fundamentally two: children (optional) and the menopause (compulsory). Men have only to worry about being a causal factor in regard to the former and on the receiving end of the latter, albeit in the latter it's at least poetic justice. Even though they don't worry about it because they rarely bother to find out about it.

Children create the need on most occasions for a career break, assuming maternity cover is available – not so for the self-employed, of course – and are a continued draw on time. That is, unless you're an author-executive, cosseted by all the support possible given the entire absence of financial constraint, suggesting that women simply "lean in" to their careers as though there were no impediments. Other approaches are available. To think that post-pandemic the LinkedIn army are mulling over the potential for people working in the office and remotely to be treated equally, when women have had to put up with this crap forever.

Being designated the primary carer in any family, resulting essentially from being the one who carried the ever-enlarging infant for 9 months and was then required to breast-feed for as long as the practice could be sustained, has given rise to what has become termed the "second shift" – the work associated with looking after a child that starts before the day job and continues after the rest of the team have adjourned to the pub for some vital offline bonding. In reality therefore it's two additional unpaid shifts. Naturally the mother gets the phone call when the infant is ill at school and has to leave to collect and takes the bulk of the leave during school holidays. In 1970 in the US women went on strike over their burden of unpaid labor[57] and were urged to write resignation letters to their partners: "You can fend for yourselves." Even today many recipients of the note wouldn't know where to even begin.

Just when the time and energy drain of childcare begins to abate comes the next sledgehammer, the unavoidable menopause: around 8 years of a jamboree bag of 40 ever-morphing symptoms that takes a tenth of women out of the workforce for good.[58] Only around a quarter of women escape with little effect at all – for three-quarters it's problematic to varying degrees. This hits women just at the time they're at the peak of their careers. Even today many are reluctant to talk about it[59] and very few men understand why their colleagues and partners have become irrational, moody, overweight and sweaty, often attributing it in ignorance to women "letting themselves go." Men have no biological excuse for finding themselves in a similar condition. It remains the last workplace taboo, which is extraordinary given that it's the single biggest wellbeing issue any organization will face. Meanwhile the 6 am yoga classes for those without childcare responsibilities and free apples for those already-knackered women, who just need a slice of cake for heaven's sake, continue. You'd think nature just didn't want women to succeed. The fact that they do is all the more impressive and admirable. That's before we've even considered how institutionally fucked is the system of work.

The cause of the ill effects of the menopause is the drop in the body of the hormone estrogen. Women have a comparatively tiny percentage of the male "pillock hormone" testosterone, too, but it's estrogen that drives the need to care, to placate, put oneself behind others. Post-menopause, the level falls to pre-pubescent levels. "Second phase" women are often therefore a different prospect altogether – determined, forceful and self-oriented. It requires men in many regards to re-learn (if they indeed ever took the time to do so first time around) what women are about. In the workplace, the difference in approach between first and second phase women is often marked. Assuming they haven't been forced to leave or had their career curtailed by the menopause.

While potentially not strictly caused by biology, the

dominance of estrogen in women in their "first phase" (pre-menopause) and their tendency to think of others before themselves goes some way toward explaining male entitlement. For it's this factor that creates so many societal and hence workplace problems. Men are used to putting themselves first and having women put them first – so where's the incentive to change? For them, the expectation of dominance pans out quite nicely.

Then there are the perceptions. Like tone of voice. The rumor was that Margaret Thatcher, the first female British Prime Minister, had her voice coached to a lower pitch during her political ascent to create a greater air of authority, but the truth seems to be that she took this on herself, almost certainly damaging her vocal cords in the process.[60] Shrill and high-pitched voices are considered to denote hysteria rather than assurance, not suitable for the exercise of power. Of course, there are cultural variations in this regard, but it's the dominant perspective globally. All of which goes a long way toward explaining the seemingly unstoppable rise of men of mediocre ability in the workplace.

History

Then we need to consider the burden of history. To say it hasn't been kind to women is an understatement. Whether it's King Mundhir's sacrifice of 400 Christian virgins to the goddess al-Uzza in what is now southern Iraq in 527, or the relentless pursuit of those suspected of witchcraft from the Middle Ages onwards, cruelty dispatched by men – often driven by their own fear – has been an all-too-common feature. Everything women have gained has been fought for and many have lost their lives doing so. All too rarely have men said, "You know, we ought to do this for women, it's the right thing."

Literature and thought speaks volumes in this regard too. There are many examples but two stand out. Arthur

Schopenhauer, revered as a philosopher of great influence, was responsible for a disgraceful diatribe, *On Women* (1851), in which he described women as "the second sex, inferior in every respect to the first."[61] He seemed to be forgiven all that, unsurprisingly, for all the other stuff. Near-fiction such as Margaret Atwood's *The Handmaid's Tale*[62] bore a striking resemblance to many aspects of the former guy's America, playing out three discrete, traditional roles for women: the subservient and mute Wives of leaders; Handmaids, perpetual birthing machines, selected and raped in what is disarmingly termed a "ceremony" for their fertility (prepared and trained by a few Aunts); and Marthas, the domestic servants. Victories were few and made little difference. Try mapping the roles to a modern organization. It's disturbingly easy.

Education

Women are schooled in subservience. It may be more subtle than when we used chalk, but it perpetuates. The expected behavior harks back to a rhyme from eighteenth-century England depicting girls as made of "sugar and spice and all things nice." They're taught silence, manners and care. Roughness and grime are considered "unbecoming" in the sense that girls will portray themselves as unsuitable partners. Bad behavior in boys, meanwhile, is considered an essential part of the exploration of their masculinity and therefore tolerated within wider boundaries. This manifests itself in the sports in which girls are encouraged to participate – netball and hockey – involving minimal physical contact and certainly no mud.

At a critical age in high school, girls often stop asking questions in class. This is particularly so in STEM subjects (science, engineering, technology and mathematics) as they're regarded as male pursuits. All too often they drop them when the opportunity arises – in the UK just under 10 percent of graduates in any of the four are women.[63] They're directed instead toward options more commonly associated with gentle domesticity.

The absence of women in the investment-rich technology field therefore is no surprise, plateauing over a decade at just 17 percent of the sector in the UK[64] despite a huge push, and 25 percent in the USA.[65] When they do arrive it's no surprise that they're greeted by male-dominated culture, causing twice as many women as men to leave the sector during the first year. All of which means that the technologies and services developed by such organizations are predominantly created and developed by men. We're all affected.

When out of education the prejudice continues. Research in 2018 showed that within the media, men are far more likely to be quoted as experts than women.[66] Qualifications, experience and achievement are still not enough to counter an innate sense that men know what they're talking about. Even if when sought, the views have to be "mansplained."

Recruitment

We haven't even passed through the revolving door yet and it's already beyond shitty. This is where in the modern age, it gets shittier. We've already mentioned that male candidates are far more likely to be selected, including by complicit women, given that women are questioned harder at interview, their achievements and credentials doubted. The most telling bias results from that which we covered first – biology. While no-one expects a role to be filled forever, a recently married woman in her early 30s appears to the recruiter, however suitable a candidate for the role, a prime candidate for near-future maternity absence. In a strange twist, due to the lack of awareness of the menopause a woman in her mid-40s is less likely to pose a conscious recruitment risk. With greater knowledge this will come.

Behavior

The recruitment process is where the first instances reveal themselves of differing gender attitudes to identical behavior, what are known as "prescriptive gender stereotypes."[67] For example, persistence in men, deemed ideally suited to advancing unpopular yet necessary change agendas or in challenging negotiations, is seen as pushiness in women, likely to irritate and alienate.

While it works in reverse too, the problem faced by women is that those characteristics deemed inherently feminine – co-operation, warmth, sensitivity, inclusiveness – aren't those associated with a historically prevalent view of leadership. Men exhibiting such behaviors are similarly prejudiced and so strain to avoid doing so. Instead of accentuating their difference, women are often drawn to emulate men. They dress in a demure, non-contentious suited fashion. But where they seek to emulate forceful male behavior as a conscious choice, believing that to win they need to play the male game, they're often penalized.

Male attributes haven't proven themselves especially viable and are unworthy of their continuing dominance. According to a study published in 2020 in Harvard Business Review, female leaders showed themselves to be far more adept at handling the Covid-19 pandemic than men[68], with inspiration, motivation, communication, collaboration and relationship building emerging as key areas required, and those in which women demonstrated superiority. The drive to equality demands that all leaders display the characteristics required to be successful, irrespective of gender. Which means re-appraising those characteristics deemed desirable for managerial and leadership roles. For the time being, despite mounting evidence, the stereotypes still present a baked-in barrier to women.

On a day-to-day basis women also have to manage the threat of predatory male behavior. Carefully constructed careers, honed over decades, can be destroyed in the rejection of an unwarranted advance from a senior male colleague. Where such drastic outcomes are avoided, reputations can be tarnished, credibility undermined. This can be the result of pursuit or of resistance, the manifestation of a personalized species-threat. While such dangers can lurk in plain sight within the sobriety of the daytime office, there's nothing to compare with the rapidly diminishing personal space of an after-hours alcohol-fueled social for full-bore danger. That's before we've got into the plethora of networking events entirely geared to male participation – spectating at sporting events (and drinking) or partaking at sports demanding of no physical prowess such as golf (and drinking afterwards). The dilemma for women is that such occasions are often where beneficial contacts are made and ideas hatched, and so to avoid them can be counterproductive. Run the gauntlet or miss out, there's no easy path for women to take.

Reward

Having put up with all the crap we've identified so far, women then find at the end of the week or month, depending on the nature of the role, their compensation is inferior to men. In the UK the gender pay gap ("the difference between average hourly earnings of men and women as a proportion of men's average hourly earnings, excluding overtime") for all employees stands at just over 15 percent.[69] For those under 40 the gap is close to zero – but fewer women move into senior management roles after this age where the pay gap widens considerably. There are, however, positive signs of this divide narrowing.

When it's all done – career, children, menopause and the battle with the prejudice associated with each – and a life of leisure beckons, retirement dishes women an even more measly share than the pay in their later years reflected. The UK pension gender gap (the percentage difference in pension income for female pensioners compared to male pensioners) stands at 40.3 percent.[70] At this stage of life there's no recourse.

Career breaks for children and care penalize women unduly in this regard. Beyond those mentioned so far, there's a second coming for nappies (the smell of which never leaves us), albeit much larger ones, and another threat to career continuity. In later years (40+) women are twice as likely as men to need to give up work to take on a full-time caring role.[71] While they may work while caring – full or (more probably) part time – the societal expectation is of women as carers. It's a thread that keeps on running.

Opportunity

Having navigated this far, wither opportunity? Organizations can effectively manage each of the challenges faced by women, should they wish to. Yet to be able to claim that opportunities are equal requires that they demonstrate success in each. An organization can't *actually be* an equal opportunities employer if it simply has a program with this aim. Nor can it claim to be when it doesn't. Which means a tiny proportion are.

Women are increasingly carving successful careers and finding senior roles, seizing or creating opportunities. They're achieving this in a manner learned over many thousands of years: a combination of determination and innate character and skill. If it were all up to men to decide, given their sense of entitlement, but for those very few who actively work to redress this ingrained inequality, little would change. Fortunately, it's increasingly not. However, the proximity bias referred to in the previous chapter threatens to stall or even reverse this advance for office-based women. They're deemed more likely to be the parent that "chooses" to remain at home to take care of children and domestic duties while their male partners escape to the comparative serenity of an all-adult environment.

Separating gender equality from the other eight characteristics, we may believe achieving equality to be impossible enough in isolation. Any of the others would have had a similar number of challenges. Yet when we consider the intersectionality – where individuals appear across several characteristics – we begin to understand the scale of the problem. We look at the single equality, diversity and inclusion (ED&I) role that's been created in many organizations and understand that it's woefully short a commitment to even beginning to consider how to dismantle the stubbornly ingrained and resistant levels of historical, institutional and shameless prejudice. All progress is to be celebrated, but if we're to un-fuck it we can't wait for increments. There's still a long, long way to go.

Having evaluated equality through the lens of gender, we do have to consider whether opportunities exist at all. Most organizations have more talent than they can grow and develop, and fewer opportunities than they can satisfy. The bottleneck breeds frustration and despondency, often turning intelligence toward negativity and deviance as it searches for an outlet. It requires conscious initiative to open channels and to equip colleagues to move through them, rather than lethargically awaiting a departure to ensure a transition. It means forgetting the rigid structure of the organization and the formality of its roles and finding expansive challenges where perhaps they were not considered. It necessitates proactivity, driving change rather than awaiting it. Fitting the opportunity to the talent and motivation, rather than the traditional opposite. We can only imagine the frustration of making huge strides to eliminate inequality and having no means for those free of its constraints to progress. While equality precedes opportunity, they need one another.

Un-f*cking inequality

Equality is a distant goal. Some have made significant strides toward it. Yet its achievement is often not solely in the gift of the organization. Embedded and solidified attitudes aren't something that can be resolved around a whiteboard. Biases are conscious and unconscious. We've become distracted with the complexities of the latter while the former continue to perpetuate, even flourish. To claim to offer equal opportunities simply cannot be true. Instead, our statement becomes:

"~~We're an equal opportunities employer~~"

"We're striving to become an equitable organization"

It's not just about opportunities – that's one aspect. It's day-to-day practices, relations and respect. So, we've replaced the phrase "equal opportunities" with "equitable." If the organization is making progress toward equality, then opportunities will be easier to identify and create, and will flow accordingly. It may still need to proactively ensure they are created, but the task becomes far easier, and the outcome more rewarding for all.

The complexities and interdependencies are significant. It's not just about being an employer, either – there will be many transient yet closely related people who will pass through an organization who deserve to be treated equally. Appointing one person and making them responsible is a start – but it's down to us all. We're all involved, We're all responsible.

There are three complementary means to un-fuck the dismal landscape of inequality in our workplaces. These are over and above the plans, projects, initiatives, ED&I roles and dubious externally published claims to having a handle on it.

The first is awareness. There's still far, far too little. It's not something a few sanitized posters and a one-day externally facilitated course will resolve. If we all understood the scale and detail of what faced us there would have been no need for this illustration. Too much of what we do know is either inherently unstructured, targeted at particular interests or pressing matters, or like jelly in a bag where we squeeze one part and another bulges. It begins to resemble four-dimensional chess when we consider the intersectionality of all types of inequality, legislated and omitted. Tracing the issues to create this short essay involved time and focus but was by no means beyond tax on a normal intellect.

With awareness we're facing the issue of whether we *want* to know. Just as an organization must want to create equality. It can seem someone else's problem, or just too mammoth a subject to even begin. The "will to knowledge" therefore needs strengthening. Rather than broadcast, most of which won't land amid the daily corporate tsunami, we do this through scenario play. Where we're not disadvantaged by inequality, we have to be placed in a hypothetical situation where it could be us. We have to prompt empathy and understanding. It's emotional immersion we need, not training. It's only by experiencing inequality, feeling the injustice it sustains, that we'll understand it. And when we understand it, we'll want to do something about it.

Second, therefore, is to create a wave of activism. There's a huge difference between being "not" something (a passive position) and being "anti" something (the taking of action). We find ourselves in double negative territory – being anti-inequality – rather than pro-equality. It's because we're opposing something, we're demanding and seeking change. Inequality is the embedded, institutionalized problem we must take down to reveal equality. The raising of awareness has to pose the question – what is it *we can do* to contribute? And then – what are we *going* to do?

Finally, from the driving of awareness and prompting and sustaining of activism, we need to share stories of achieving equality. That is, all stories, positive and negative, freely and without accusation, across all areas of inequality and not just those subject to current focus. Our own world, our limited experiences are insufficient to ensure that we learn quickly enough, for we have much ground to cover. They cannot be weaponized or used to hold our colleagues to account. Where we're unsighted, haven't considered the ramifications of our action or inaction, where we forget ourselves, we need to know. Perhaps this even prompts starting every meeting or interaction with sharing such stories, while ensuring that there's an accessible and evolving repository for our learning. For leaders and managers will need to relinquish all control over such stories, seeing them as the collective property of the organization even where they're attached in some way to themselves. It's important not to anonymize them, too, helping build safety within an organization. Equality belongs to us all.

Chapter 7

"Culture eats strategy for breakfast"

Only it doesn't. Does it?

It's extraordinary when something that's supposedly been with humankind since we first awoke after a night of restless dreams under a bush in the Olduvai Gorge continually escapes definition. Few fields of writing in the organizational domain are more taxing than that associated with attempting to define, model and explain culture. Yet we use the expression constantly because we feel we have enough of a general sense of what it means. Or, rather, what we believe it means. It's been used already in this book.

We can search every dusty corner of sociology and anthropology looking for something that works and inevitably emerge on each occasion laden with another 400 pages of closely typed and heavily referenced caveat, nuance and contradiction that no amount of stabbing ourselves in the thigh with a sharp pencil can assuage. We seem habitually prone to edging further away from something workable with every attempt. Placing the term "organizational" in front of culture doesn't seem to narrow it down any.

Strategy, on the other hand, is simple. It's what we're going to do, why we're going to do it, how we're going to do it, when we're going to do it and what we need to be able to do it. Yet it's the junior partner according to the opening statement. The focus here, therefore, will be on what's eating it.

It feels almost inevitable that another alleged Druckerism is our provocation. With no evidence of him having actually said it, Drucker offered a lot else around the subject by way of helpful clarification. It's been suggested that the closest reference to this actual statement appeared in the September 2000 issue of the trade journal *North American Papermaker: The Official Publication of the Paper Industry Management Association*[72], of which we can naturally all reach for a copy. That it channeled Drucker has left us with the ironically nauseating suggestion of a lot of things consuming a lot of things for three square meals a day. It also implies that the consumed item in each case is no more, chewed, digested and the waste jettisoned. Those aspects of the gastric process don't appear to have been thought through. All the more reason to dismantle the idea.

To wander aimlessly in the garden of arcane delight[73] for a few moments, we can admire the attempt at a snappy catch-all routed by the crisp white shirts of McKinsey, specifically Marvin Bower, as in "the way we do things around here.[74]" It is, at least, plain speaking. As most commercial organizations don't lend themselves naturally to communitarian principles or instincts, it's more likely to actually mean "the way we're told to do things around here." It also implies a static state of *being*, our ways chipped in stone, rather than the reality of ever evolving *becoming*. Perhaps it's intentional. Change is risk, and culture can't be put at risk.

Many look upon culture as a collection of interrelated components such as history, art, belief, ritual, architecture, social habits and expression, the sum of which is a way of life. Culture as understood in this way is visible in our behavior and our creations. Hence, we believe we see it as a tangible "thing."

It depends how you frame what you see, and the emotional prompts it engenders. Where there's visibility there's interpretation. While an individual depiction of a culture is distinctly possible, a shared understanding is problematic. It leaves us with a natural tendency to aggregate for ease of comprehension. Like an extended word cloud, if you'd like to imagine this is a presentation. We're in the same quaggy territory as values, ideas that we supposedly share but struggle to define, let alone align. If enough people mention Morris Dancing, for example, then it's in, even if there are other clearer, more meaningful and less terrifying contributions available. To create a shared sense of belonging, therefore, a generous helping of generalization is needed. It's rather ironic that in doing so we drive out the curiosities and oddities that would otherwise make it compelling. In trying to interpret culture, therefore, we have a tendency to kill it.

Yet we might believe we see ghosts too. A rather absorbing argument was made by the geographer Don Mitchell in 1995[75] that culture doesn't exist *as a thing*, only as the idea of a thing formed under certain historical conditions. People behave, however, as though there's such a thing. Emerging from this proposition is culture as a means of division and control, a force against change even though the very idea of culture is subject to influences that evolve it. Effectively therefore those with power get to decide what culture is, how it gets represented, who is within it and who is outside. It takes our interpretation of Bower a step further into the darkness. But imagine how powerful a proposition this is for the leadership of an organization, and how abhorrent for everyone else within it.

Some try to balance this with a petalized mode. "The Cultural Web" devised by Gerry Johnson and Kevan Scholes is just such.[76] It gives equal credence to stories, rituals and symbols as it does to the organizational structure and systems that channel power and control to itself. At the center is "The Paradigm" or model of the working environment. Also, a nightclub in Groningen, in the Netherlands. Yet it's unlikely they can ever be equal, such is the dominance in most organizations of systems and structures in shaping stories, symbols and rituals. Where cultural deficiencies are revealed, the solution offered to their redress is change management. Where the solution to *anything at all* is change management, we're in more trouble than we realize.

We therefore arrive at a juncture.

On the one branch, culture as a definable, knowable positive force for change, and one that's itself "praxis" (practice, rather than theory) as sociologist Zygmunt Bauman described[77], perpetually becoming. Drucker didn't regard strategy as inferior to culture, but held that a positive, evident and supportive culture was a vehicle for success. Like a vacuum tube.

On the other branch, culture as constraint, conformity and coercion. Constraint in defining the boundaries of acceptability. Conformity in establishing that remaining within those limits makes for an easier and more comfortable life even if we'd rather be doing something else. Coercion kicking in where the other two fail and a breach occurs.

Some have considered that where we have landed culturally is a summation of the courage, exploits, intellect, vision and all-round derring-do of a smattering of those we can but envy. Culture more, therefore, a reflective outcome than a force. The "great man theory" found its clearest expression in Thomas Carlyle's 1841 series of essays *On Heroes, Hero-Worship, and The Heroic in History*[78]. Their shaping of our world has through history taken a number of paths: king, poet, priest, philosopher and prophet, amongst others. Not thought leader or futurist, thankfully. But there are many still prepared – often quietly – to believe in its thesis.

Throughout history, experiments in attempting to proactively create a consciously superior culture haven't ever ended well. Fortunately. Yet in many societies a sense of exceptionalism pervades. Culture is a tool of competition too. Our writers are better than yours, our food is more refined, our cities are more beautiful and their streets safer because we're *better people*. The teaching of history, a major contributor to the idea of culture, tends in each society to focus primarily on its own: its heroes, wars, conquests, art, inventions. And in expressing its elevation, its lasting gifts to the world. Like Morris Dancing. Organizations are prone to the same tendency. In many respects these efforts reinforce the notion of a suitably supportive culture being a vehicle for the effective execution of strategy.

Sub-cultures and diversity

There are two natural forces heaving their shoulder against the reality or idea of a definable culture – sub-cultures and diversity. We'll consider the subbies first. Sometimes referred to as tribes by those who still make tomahawks out of sticks, not just for fun. Whether it's the Amish in Ohio or punks in London's Kings Road, groups with identifiable beliefs, rituals and identity exist within a broader "parent" culture without associating with it and in some cases actively rejecting it. Their number, complexity and occasional overlap serve to undermine the homogeneity and hence definability of the parent.

Some consider sub-cultures to be simply harmless dressing up. This is reflected in many instances in the sporadic nature of allegiance. The character known as the "Ace Face" in the 1979 film *Quadrophenia*, idolized for his razor-sharp style, carefree disregard for authority and freewheeling spirit by his followers, is revealed at the film's end to be a forelock-tugging hotel bell boy by day. The genre is also mocked in the 1978 song *Part Time Punks* by the British band Television Personalities – "they pogo in their bedroom, in front of the mirror, but only when their Mum's gone out." They're sometimes seen as an existential threat to those from whom they're different, as though the offspring might consume the parent, manifesting in verbal and even physical threat or attack.[79] Yet the eventual absorption of sub-cultures into the mainstream is part of what creates organic social stability, a natural evolutionary process that allows ideas to be surfaced, considered and accepted. A kind of socially stabilizing fail-fast fail-often strategy.

The existence of sub-cultures is one among several reasons to counter the somewhat lazy assertion that culture is the "operating system" of the organization, setting rules and boundaries and allowing "apps" (people and processes) to function. An organizational culture isn't a closed loop, it's integrated with its environment, feeding it and fed by it. It's emergent rather than designed and organized; cajoled, prompted and challenged rather than maintained and upgraded; unpredictable and surprising, not expected and dry. Not an operating system then. At all.

We ought to distinguish sub-cultures from silos, the beasts that every management consultant hunts with a blunt instrument and can usually find blindfolded. While sub-cultures create an identity, consciously or subconsciously, they're usually more than capable of working constructively and openly with one another as dominance isn't an objective. If anything, they shy away from it, passively resisting the absorption that hegemony would bring. Silos on the other hand are departments or groups that form to resist transparency and engagement, motivated by fear-based protectionism. There's usually a paranoid manager circling the wagons. They may at times accidentally comprise some of those who identify with sub-cultures, but silos are rarely culturally defined.

When considering culture within organizations much of what we've covered exists as a microcosm. Professions create sub-cultures, most notably where they ascribe to an institutionalized methodology such as Agile. Scrums, tribes (there we go again), stand-ups, pair working and even dress style (or conscious rejection of) ensure the group are identifiable. They coalesce, partly by virtue of working together, partly for comfort. They talk their own quasi-language, accentuating its difference from the normal lingua. Other sub-cultures are more accidental, entangled in jargon and processes that sustain separateness while often attempting to integrate. Some, meanwhile, feel the need to professionally distance, such as Human Resources, forever caught in the void between the needs and concerns of "people" and wishing to sit on the shoulders of senior leadership as "business partners." And then somehow managing to not be trusted or appreciated for the valuable work they do by either. Organizational sub-cultures also exist geographically. Workplaces in different locations will develop their own recognizable patterns of behavior and rituals, even in the same country yet especially marked across geographical boundaries. Even down to the way they perceive the organization itself and their colleagues. This is particularly marked where an operation has been subsumed as part of a corporate acquisition, where changing the livery on the factory gates is deemed effective assimilation. Many a corporate apparatchik has discovered to their reputational cost that a centrally conceived initiative has a variable chance of success across disparate locales, and that a mandate can account for little. "We're from head office" can be tantamount to an invitation to be metaphorically tarred and feathered. And so, it operates as a complex matrix, "horizontal" professional and occupational adhesion with "vertical" locational stakes in the soil.

Then we have diversity, a simple fact of most modern societies across a broad range of actualities (the way people are) and preferences (the way they wish to be). We focused on this in the previous chapter on equality, yet it's relevant here too. Aside from being relevant everywhere, of course. While there may be a tendency in some instances toward coalescence of those of a similar nature in either physical locality, shared agendas or overt sub-cultures, this isn't always the case. Where it is, it's often because they too can be treated in a similar manner to sub-cultures, as a threat to control, morality or continuity. They collect for safety. Very often, though, diversity is scattered, creating a broader, more enriched idea of culture within a country or area. Degrees of assimilation and harmonization can make identifying the nature and level of diversity difficult, particularly given its dynamic nature. Yet all the while it's eating into the idea of a singular identifiable culture, enriching the entirety.

Diversity adds to the "horizontal" complexity. The intent to include is driven by recruitment policies and preferences, a specific and articulated desire to ensure a broad spectrum of difference in the workforce, as far as possible attaining a position of balance. More difficult still, having assembled such an array, is providing and maintaining – as we focused on – equality of opportunity. This is usually where it falls over. Resistance remains largely institutionalized across industry. Prejudice and practice formed over decades, if not millennia, have proven incredibly difficult to dismantle. Very often people are hired for their difference and there remain *because of* their difference. An honest advertisement for such roles would shamefully say: "We need you for our stats but don't expect to get anywhere."

Organizational norms and behaviors all too often reflect a simple factor – the path to success. If being honest, decent and caring is seen to be the way we get on in an organization, we'll ensure it's how we're known and seen. If being a completely amoral soul-stripped shit is how we advance at the expense of all others and their limpid feelings, then we'll crack on with a whip in both fists. We have a choice, of course: comply or rebel. Compliance is easier but there's more competition. Rebellion offers more open ground but it's far more exposed. Whichever way, the definition of culture becomes "it's how we get somewhere around here."

From all of this we're asked to make sense of "organizational culture."

Cultural breakdown

What makes this so galling for us goes right back to the idea of culture eating strategy for breakfast, as a hand often played. While it may be tough to admit it, in isolation it's disposable. Yet it's managed all on its own to convince organizational leadership that the *creation* of a suitable culture is both possible and achievable. The fundamental error at the heart of almost every initiative intended to affect culture, beyond every consideration mentioned so far, is that as Bauman suggested it's in constant flux, impacted by an unpredictable and varying array of forces and features. To consider that culture can be tinkered with like a car engine, adding a dash of lube and perhaps tightening a few nuts, is a delusion that has afflicted many. Yet we all get drawn into these gargantuan, disorienting initiatives. Ironically, very often we're asked to try and influence outcomes over which we have no control at the expense of those that we do, notably strategic preparation, planning and delivery. The stuff that supposedly got eaten for breakfast.

It's often the perpetrators of the relations, agendas, behaviors and practices interpreted as culture who are calling them out as unacceptable and attempting to alter them as they struggle to understand why their leadership is eating itself. As established, the acts and omissions of leaders define the boundaries of what's acceptable within the organization. Where an organization has at last recognized it needs to take steps to re-shape its relations, extracting a toxic ego is often the singularly most constructive act of cultural renewal possible. It's one of the few interventions necessary in this regard. Far more cathartic and instant than a company-wide "great leap forward." Both symbolically and in practice. A few opportunistic sycophants will be sorry and seek out a new role model, no-one else.

This is no revelation. Yet we don't like to talk about it. It's not like we don't see this on a day-to-day basis. We know from where the problem flows. We know the way it flows. We know those who feed from it, as it serves their purposes or makes their life easier. And we know where and how it hides – behind achievement. Results. The ends turning a blind eye to the means. We're back to bullying again. There's no justification sought or needed. Culture becomes, "It's the way I do things around here.

If you don't like it, you can bugger off."

Then we get the forced change, pressed through a sieve, usually in the hands of a business function that's deemed can't possibly do too much damage. Which means the fringe is tasked with re-making the center. None is more nauseating and destined to have the entirely opposite effect than the drive to have "fun at work."

Fun at work as we normally understand it is natural, incidental, unpredictable, beautiful when it happens. It's spontaneous and organic. It's one of the facets of work that makes it tolerable, even at times desirable. Yet making it something that needs to happen for our benefit is beyond artificial. We're presented with the same turd that gets rolled in glitter for every non-core corporate initiative – productivity, wellbeing, engagement, trust, satisfaction, attraction and retention. What began with a foosball table in the corner for recalcitrant males has become an entire flowery-shirted industry that announces "work is fucked" with a kazoo.

Fun at work has become the neo-opiate of the people, complete with its own library of glazed and confused stock photos to helpfully explain what having fun *looks like*. Committed atheist Karl Marx (him, again), of course, originally had this down as religion – "the sigh of the oppressed creature, the heart of a heartless world, and the soul of soulless conditions.[80]" Yet he hadn't reckoned on mandatory shots of tequila from plastic cows.[81] Because when it's forced, the opposite happens. Some have tried to create a "model" of fun at work, blending the accidental with the planned[82], an apology for something best buried in an unmarked grave. Others have even gone so far as to create a permanent Head of Fun role, ensuring that like the film *The Blair Witch Project*, there's no escape from the horror.

Objecting to these approaches isn't comfortable. We're marked out as serious, dull, gray. As Karl Marx is often portrayed; we don't know, he could have been one for late nights and the *craic*. We're scorned for not wanting to enjoy ourselves when we just don't want to be told to enjoy ourselves. We're goofing on command when we actually want challenge, learning, development, opportunities, collegiality, autonomy, inspiration. And, of course, dialog, to be listened to, rather than force-fed kindergarten puree. Compulsory clowning is intervention, interruption, often downright humiliation, and we'll do almost anything to avoid it. Increased levels of working from home for many since the outbreak of Covid-19 have provided the perfect excuse not to have to dress up. At least not their off-camera bottom half. Because dressing up is what sub-cultures do voluntarily. As a means of definition, expression and intent. Not to announce that they're an arse – there were other signs of this trait, it didn't just suddenly reveal itself in a gibbon outfit.

We also have to acknowledge that "fun at work" began in the male domain and has essentially persisted within it. Most of the kit of fun remains masculine and juvenile – slides, climbing walls, foosball, table tennis, gaming consoles, ball pits. All designed with a Silicon Valley subculture attire in mind. Because much of this came from the domain of key-press engineering and cornflakes three times a day. For many years it's been an excessively gender-imbalanced environment, mirroring the essentially patriarchal education system where the boys make useless crap with welding torches in metalwork while girls safely bake butterfly cakes. This before we even get close to other forms of diversity that are entirely at odds with fun-at-work programs rendering them just another manifestation of inequality in which the organizational willingly invests while inanely claiming the opposite.

Un-f✳cking culture

There's something of the dynamic of the playground about attempting to entirely subjugate one idea to another. In this case the ideas are so fundamentally different that comparison is absurd. While the headline statement has been clarified on numerous occasions, as is often the case the explanation often falls away leaving only the headline for misinterpretation. An organization without cultures would find strategy impossible to develop and implement; an organization with vibrant and supportive cultures without strategy will veer drunkenly onto the rocks in a contended haze. The essential presence of both therefore has our statement become:

"~~Culture eats strategy for breakfast~~"

"Culture makes strategy possible, strategy channels culture"

The two are of equal importance because they do different essential and essentially different things. We can use this approach to the re-statement of other ideas wherever the breakfast analogy is used, until perhaps the table is cleared, and its disappearance is no longer noticed.

At the heart of what's considered "culture" lay three approaches to un-fucking our misplaced belief in its all-consuming dominance and conviction that we can create a singular version of culture that suits our agenda.

First, we're "excellent to each other." It's an idea that found blissfully innocent expression in the 1989 film *Bill and Ted's Excellent Adventure*, a simple mantra, but extremely difficult to practice. Prior to this it was woven through history, but never so beautifully captured. If we're simply decent to one another, respect and honor our shared interests, understand that we're all fighting our own personal battles and that those struggles may occasionally surface in the very act of being human, work would be better for us all. It means slowing down, considering whether what we do or don't do, say or don't say, will be helpful or cause harm, while allowing others their vulnerability. It's on us all. It's the pre-requisite for the rest. Which means it should probably be at the beginning of the book. And in every chapter.

Second, we pursue diversity with every breath, affording every opportunity, dispensing with the fabrication that is "fit." The broader the base for our relations, the greater the number of perspectives, influences and interpretations, and the less inclination will exist to force the idea of a singular culture into an ever-narrower sea-lane. Fit is a fearful proposition, limitation and constraint, a bunker mentality that has no place in corporate life. Sub-cultures should be given freedom to express in order to drive greater understanding, as through such they can help enlighten and enrich us all. We need to remain conscious of not getting into the inevitable "breaking down silos" territory where sub-cultures are concerned. It can be a fine line, on one side of which we flourish, on the other side of which we invite more centralized control and are all thereby diminished.

Third, with our commitment to excellence toward one another and pursuit of diversity, we're able to recognize, understand and celebrate the multiple cultures within our organization and avoid the temptation to try and engineer the dominance of any one. Or to even believe in, or advocate, the aim or the possibility. It allows less desirable cultural traits and behaviors – such as those covered in Chapter 4 – to surface and dissipate. The aim is not their suppression, as a certain misguided romance can become attached, but their natural passing. In doing so we thereby avoid the temptation to ascribe dominance to a concept we struggle to understand and define and expect this will be beneficial in any way at all. It enables us to avoid the breakfast analogy altogether. From this point on and for all time. Nothing consumes anything. Which helps us resist trying to force fit culture through endless corporate initiatives that instead serve to ridicule, undermine and destroy it. There are often simple, if awkward, localized fixes to what are deemed cultural problems, without having to try and re-make the whole in order to avoid facing up to them.

The idea of culture will perpetuate. The world of work is one of the interplay of a myriad of cultures, from the evident and vibrant to the emergent to those just beginning to form. Some will be conceived in opposition to those that appear to dominate. Their interplay is a thing of beauty. To be admired – and left alone. We have enough to do.

Chapter 8

"If it ain't broke, don't fix it"

So, we don't. Do we?

We're ideas machines. We generate, process and churn them out at quite an incredible rate. Like frogspawn, most won't survive the first few minutes. That's one in fifty, which is probably generous. Many, of course, are ridiculous, but if every idea was good, we'd be crushed under the weight of our own genius.

We have over 6000 thoughts a day, so it seems.[83] Thoughts aren't ideas as such, not all could potentially lead to the emergence of something tangible or new. While our brains are popping and fizzing like fireworks in a bag of matches, we can be assured in the workplace we're entirely surrounded by an army of mains-connected hose-wielders programmed to preserve and conserve. And so, each day begins anew the constant struggle of cognitive sparks to ignite and break before they're doused and forgotten. Commentary by David Attenborough.

The opening phrase is widely attributed[84] to T. Bert (Thomas Bertram) Lance, the Director of the Office of Management and Budget in Jimmy Carter's 1977 administration, albeit it appeared to be in colloquial use prior to this. It was essentially a cost saving plea. Yet he did also add that government had an equal and opposite habit of not fixing things that *were* broken. And so, the test was "brokenness." Its simplicity created a lasting appeal, sitting warmly in the hearts today of those who can't be bothered to look at something. Columnist William Safire wrote in the 1990s that it "has become a source of inspiration to anti-activists."[85] We'll deal with the uninspired in due course.

But the phrase makes no logical sense. Which, of course, could have been its witty intent. To "fix" something is to repair it. A need is an essential pre-requisite. Something that isn't broken doesn't need to be repaired. A repair is in such instances an impossibility. The actual argument being offered is if something appears to be working then don't bother spending time improving it or risk breaking it. It implies (but doesn't state) that we should look for the things that aren't working properly and improve them instead. On this basis we can envisage a perfect world where eventually everything is functioning as intended, nothing is broken, and our work is done.

Therein lies another problem – how do we know if something's working? What's "working" for me may not be for you: my role could be to stop you doing something you want – even need – to do. It may be working enough to get by. It may be only delivering on a fraction of its capability, like all the software commonly used in our endeavors. Most processes in the workplace are only partially effective and efficient. Most workplaces too.

Which means that most of the improvements we pursue aren't so much about increased functionality but workarounds. Things we can do to avoid having to do what we've been told is the approved or the given "best way" to do something. Because even if well intentioned and sensible at the time of implementation they're usually glitchy at best, downright shocking at the grunt end. And in the complex adaptive system in which they reside, everything else with which they interface and interact has changed. We're practical creatures. Just like non-creative beasts with whom we share the planet, we initiate and follow "desire lines" that connect two points in the shortest, safest manner, trampling the vegetation as we go to show the others. When the path we've trodden no longer works for us, we find and tread another.

Kaizen

Continual improvement – or the disguise worn by the specific and intentional circumvention of the paralyzing bureaucracy with which we're often saddled – has its own proud corporate philosophy. "Kaizen" is a Japanese term meaning "change for the better." Why anyone would actually set out to "change for the worse" is a worthy question, even when despite good intent it ends up that way. It's one of those things that has surely existed since humankind first plowed a field, but corporate philosophies weren't much use then. Yet in its modern incarnation, like the Ritz Hotel, it's supposedly open to all employees.

The small-step improvement approach began in the Training Within Industry (TWI) program in the US during World War Two, in which no-one had time for unwieldy resource-voracious projects. It ended up being exported to Japan under the Marshall Plan to help the US rebuild those industries it had succeeded in flattening. In spirit at least, the idea of iterative improvement embodied within was the underlying prompt for the creation of the Agile methodology in 2001. Software development theorists can get very testy about these things, but essentially it was an approach that broke down large projects into small, regularly appraised short-run stints. It welcomed change as a friend rather than locking it out, keeping quiet and pretending it would go away.

So, is continuous improvement open to everyone? Only if the organization lets it be. Which entails knowing what it is and means, believing it's a good idea and creating the two-way channels needed for it to work and ensuring the measures and resources are available to act accordingly. A lot of assumptions, all of which must be true in both theory and practice. That's at least ten chances to get it wrong or break the essential loop.

Evolution

Evolution in the natural world simply occurs. It has no aims or goals, it rolls on, as change is, literally, everything. It's a race against time with no end, in which the only rule is adapt to the changing environment or it's the early bath of extinction. Some have managed to do the barest minimum, like the goblin shark, which has let 125 million years drift by without too much effort.[86] The corporate world can't wait for its lumbering beasts to slither from the swamp and grow legs. It relies on them being aware of what's necessary and driving the required changes themselves. To do so, it needs ideas.

Those of us that are old enough to remember the hyper-analog workplace will recall the delights of the "suggestions box." It's understood to have been first introduced in 1890 by Daniel W. Voorhees, a US Senator from Indiana and called a "petitions box." It was basically an early form of crowdsourcing.

The suggestions box was often a small cardboard container, helpfully covered by a willing apparatchik in domestic floral wallpaper for effect, in which anyone could post an idea, either with their name on or anonymously. Amid the chocolate bar wrappers and betting slips was occasionally a keeper, but for the most part its contribution was as a sign: "We want to hear from our people." Whether or not they actually did.

It's one of those features of the analogue world that never made the transition to the digital, despite being an obvious candidate. The assumption being that if someone had an idea, they would just drop someone an (auditable) email. Yet the suggestions box was the introvert's friend. It helped those who were uncomfortable in a public domain to offer an idea for consideration without having to raise their hand in a meeting, or even pitch it across a table. It also aided those who were too shy to be associated with their idea. Paradoxically, at the same time the floral boxes began disappearing, organizations were becoming increasingly focused on the necessity for continual improvement. However, without a physical repository there was no clear and visible method.

It's quite likely – albeit the assertion is made without evidence, hard to now come by – that listening to their people and doing something positive in response may well have saved or at least prolonged the likes of Blockbuster, Woolworths, Toys "R" Us, Borders, Kodak, MFI, Polaroid, MySpace, Friends Reunited, Maplin, Netscape, Comet and many others whose "innovation lag" (a polite expression for something altogether more problematic) ensured their demise. Unsurprisingly, we've managed quite well in their absence, with the possible exception of Woolworth's, without whom the sourcing of chocolate bars the size of a mortuary slab (and a ticket for part of the way) has become problematic.

There have, of course, surfaced plenty of examples – mostly myth – of innovation from the shop floor, in which an hourly-paid provider of hardy labor has managed to see what was invisible through the top floor coin-slot telescope. From doubling the size of toothpaste tube holes to bottling fizzy drinks to removing the strike pad from one side of a matchbox. In some of these stories the canny salt-of-the-earth holds back and negotiates a sizable fee before disclosure, in others they innocently gift it for told-you-so kudos and an acknowledging, half-hearted pat on the back. We love these rare moments of unsuspecting yet startling clarity, particularly when ransomed. They feel like proletarian justice. Until we realize it's the same accumulist game everyone's playing, using the hand we're dealt.

Activism

We promised earlier we'd consider the activists and their antithesis. Activism is the use of vigorous and directed campaigning to engender political or social change. We step into the sphere when we cease to be merely pro or contra something as a matter of policy or belief and start doing something about it. Even if it's stuffing leaflets in letterboxes, marching with a banner or lobbying an employer for something that to us genuinely means something. The formation of LGBTQ+ (Lesbian, Gay, Bisexual, Transexual and Queer) groups within organizations was one such area. It took committed activism to ensure they were created, endorsed and resourced. The collective momentum has ensured they are now expected and respected. Most such activism has a ratchet effect.

Activists in this way want to change things "for the better." It's not part of their job, but they believe it to be right and necessary. As such it often comes with high risk. They often see something as broken which others don't consider to be. Because, vitally, as we established "broken" can be a matter of perspective or interpretation and in the absence of objectivity it becomes a battle centered on its control. Un-fucking work is itself an activism. This book is, after all, a rambling campaign pamphlet whose aim is to turn you, the reader, into a similarly motivated agitator. Or what's it for? If you put it down and don't pick up a cause, we've failed. We're trying to change work for the better. For good.

Yet we're also aware of the possible danger lurking within activism. A critic known in anarchist circles as Andrew X notes: "The activist role is a self-imposed isolation from all the people we should be connecting to."[87] That is, a conscious aloofness. The argument runs that we become burdened by the role and in defining ourselves in this manner we impede our ability to achieve the change we desire. It's a libertarian's curious argument for greater personal liberty in the struggle for collective liberty. It appears to lead nowhere useful.

At the other end of the bell curve, we have the cheery un-activists. The term isn't as we'd imagine it, a reference to the committed lethargist – it's a conscious position, distinct from the non-activist. They're the standard bearers for T. Bert Lance's dictum, formidable in their commitment to not being arsed in case it creates more or different demands. Strangely, while often being entirely and often vocally dissatisfied with their work they're hell-bent on preserving it. As if it were entirely theirs to do with as they please. They're harmless until they accidentally find their way through the myriad fault lines in the organization into mid-ranking and senior positions in which they have the scope to influence the present and future, and thereby resolutely elect not to. Until history washes over them like the tide. Sometimes they take the entire organization with them into the undertow. It's a planetary waste of opportunity. We always seem to know who they are.

Finally we have the anti-activists, those who attempt to discredit, disrupt and derail an activism. They're not by default conservative, as their motivation may be the negation of what's considered to be a regressive cause. Their target isn't an issue, but those in pursuit of an issue.

Most of us are not activist, un-activist or anti-activist, but poised cautiously between. Where a cause for change exists, we inactively support or reject it. The most we might manage is a social media post or two, a "like" if we'd rather not say anything. We're conscious of both the time burden and the risks of activism, especially so within our employment where the margins for exit are far narrower than they might be within broader society. Which is to a significant degree why work remains fucked. Because we have through historical inaction, in this area as with many others we've covered, been – and remain – complicit. Yet it's at the same time understandable. We have much to lose, for ourselves and our dependents. As any social activist would tell us, "the system" (as in, everything) is stacked against us. Which is the very nature of systems. They're intended to control, restrict and contain. If it's not stacked against us it's probably not a system so we don't really need to waste time being frustrated by it or protesting it. Employment by its very nature is no different. So, when we see that something can be improved, we use the available channels, formal and informal, to influence it, treading softly, whispering until it feels safe to speak.

Not being arsed

Which brings us to the first, glaring horror of a stasis-oriented organization – simply being there at all. Observing and being subject to persistent problems, whether inefficiency, unfairness, inequality, homogeneity or prejudice, and watching those who might do something to address them either deny their existence or accept them and elect not to act. The delusion of the insignificance or unimportance of such issues is often shared. It needs to be, such is it that one person alone couldn't hold back the swell of changing attitudes and expected norms. Invariably if it's happening in one corner, it's happening in them all. In the natural world, creatures that don't evolve the means to survive in a changing environment are swallowed by it. A quiet passage into the folklore of corporate failure is often the kindest route for their ilk. The only solution for us is to get out. Fast. We'll set them aside, as they'll surely manage to do for themselves.

Ideas often get confused with innovation. Organizations love innovation because they can generally sell it, either into an existing market or to create a new one. They're right to. It's the ticket to tomorrow. Ideas aren't the same as innovation. They might lead to innovation if developed effectively. They might instead solve a problem, make something easier, simpler or cheaper, or remove a barrier. Organizations love to think of themselves as innovative and paint the word on the wall or twist it in neon to remind everyone that they have to be, or it's goodbye. Other than in a crisis, like trying to return Apollo 13 safely to Earth, you can't force it, however brightly the script in the staff café twinkles.

For the bearer of an idea, whether as a formless momentary spark or fertilized, incubated and fully formed yet helpless and dependent infant, the path to its recognition as a thought of value within the organization is like that facing a newly hatched turtle from the dunes to the waterline. We know all too well that only a few make it – but those that do must then sustain the next iteration of the slow predator-dodging front crawl of progress. The risks are many. Rejection, misappropriation, discreditation and even humiliation await. That's because there's a potential value in an idea like no other asset we recognize. They are humanity's most precious commodity. They require no inputs or resources beyond those that the body requires to simply survive in complete disengagement. And there are no clues whatsoever that the bearer might display to suggest for a moment that it is they who are the chosen one. Indeed, if it's us, we often haven't got a clue either.

One of the most dismal responses to an idea is disinterest. Investment of any time whatsoever in the corporate world is an opportunity cost. To look at *this* means to stop working on *that*. And if we stop working on *that* and *this* doesn't work then we'll be even further behind with *that* and there'll probably be *the other* to do as well. There's undoubtedly personal risk lurking in such a cumulative deposit of expectation. We'll be answerable for our judgment. This scenario presents probably the single biggest reason why new technologies are almost always evaluated later than the need for them demands. It's workload. When we consider as we did earlier in this meditation that the vast majority of what lies piled in the "in tray" is noise, essentially, we're not interested in ideas because we've got stuff to do that probably doesn't need, or isn't worth, doing but is required to be. Being interested in, and willing to listen to, ideas is, however, the entire reason we're there. So, when our idea gets biffed for a pile of emails and a monthly report and a compliance training session, it's the ultimate proof of our irrelevance. And we'll do it to others, too. We're just as likely to be the purveyor of faintly hassled ignorance as those around us.

Another response of equal and opposite horror is the rapid escalation of our idea into a "project" complete with cunningly random codename and a cast of extras that would shame Bollywood, Hollywood and Nollywood combined. We're forced to bear witness to the beauty and innocence of our suggestion being transformed into a terrifying, all-consuming beast, our kitten into a Minotaur. We move at pace away from the intent of the idea toward a bold re-statement of the aim, one with an identity and purpose of its own that we no longer recognize. Because organizations love creating projects and people love to be associated with a winner. Everyone will want to be involved, at the meetings, on the calls, doing their utmost to try and contribute, so they can say they did. Until it all appears to have veered into quicksand and then no-one will have even heard of it.

For all this intent we show to create and deliver improvement, recognition is often fleeting and scant. For most of us, we lack the market-stall savvy of the shop floor genius who doesn't declare until the reward is negotiated. We're innately unentrepreneurial. We're dutiful, obedient souls who see our path to greatness sanctioned by management and inked onto our HR record that gets filed beyond retrieval when we leave. We may get a small increase in bonus, a one-time spot award like a couple of cinema tickets, or a special call-out during the Monday morning team meeting or our annual appraisal. Organizations who claim to value innovation can be just as equally appalling at recognizing those who spawn it. That's because it's expected. It's in the manual and on the wall. Our employment contract secures organizational ownership of the intellectual property (IP) we generate. It's why there are "brainstorm rooms" and "think hubs" all over the workplace. It's what we do. It's why we joined, to work with a progressive company that boldly makes stuff happen. Every idea is expected to be followed by another, because we're living the values. After the high fives, we've nowhere to go with our disappointment. We signed up for it.

Un-f✱cking apathy

The opening statement is a convenience, a disposable line

perhaps appropriate in a garden workshop yet adopted as a corporate mantra where avoidance appears preferable to evolution. Yet evolution isn't a choice when nothing else stands still. Our statement therefore adapts, too:

"~~If it ain't broke, don't fix it~~"

"If it's broken we make it good, if it's good we make it better"

We don't need a plan, because there will be stuff we don't know; we need to be prepared. To have the right mindset. To be open. It's part of that responsibility to ourselves and others. Because sometimes it may be us that's broken.

Having made a bed of nettles for ourselves and been helpfully tucked up and in by the organization, three possible ways to help us un-fuck the reluctance to harness ideas in the workplace are as follows.

First, we have to see and recognize ideas for the unique currency that they are, rather than an inconvenience that will ensure we remain mired in our present helplessness. That includes those that appear far-fetched, misguided, irrelevant and ridiculous through the smeared lens of today. Those that bring us ideas care enough to do so. We therefore need to care enough to listen, and to adjust our view. So that when we have an idea we're listened to. It's self-perpetuating. Which means, fundamentally, there are no bad or ridiculous ideas. There are those that become useful and those that were perhaps not of their time but may yet come again. If they don't, they at least found airspace and were heard.

So, there must be a channel for them to be aired, pitched, suggested. Beyond the floral wallpapered box or its digital reincarnation, or the usual overcrowded paths. Which further means there has to be a response mechanism within the channel that fully and clearly indicates that the idea has been listened to. They need an appropriate recognition and reward structure. Some respond to the former, some the latter, but it should include both to be certain. We're employees, we don't do it for love despite the buffed smiles the stock photos depict. Least of all for anonymous shareholders. It has the same negative connotations as the "discretionary effort" referenced in Chapter 3. If everywhere we take ideas feels like exploitation, we'll keep them to ourselves. After all, we don't need to say anything at all, our eyes won't give it away, no-one will ever know what might have been but us. Or we'll take them somewhere we'll be listened to.

Second, we have to recognize that the blunt instrument of a project can potentially be the worst mode of transport for an idea, an off-peak single to oblivion. While there will clearly be times where this is needed – scale, urgency for example – we must dispense with the tendency to drop every thought of potential worth into the unforgiving corporate machinery of a formal mandate, roles and a timeline. Sometimes an idea needs time to nurture, to run different paths. We have to turn it over in our hands. It may not be what we first think. That involves experimentation, the setting loose of "Trojan mice"[88] – small changes that can be assessed and tweaked, with no worry that they might not succeed, that may in turn spawn other ideas or clarify our original thought. When the time comes to turn the idea into a reality, the carriage we choose may be very different. Of course, it may not, but at least we'll be choosing it for the right reason, rather than habit.

Third, we must maintain a restless curiosity and deploy critical thinking in respect of everything we encounter in the course of our work. We should accept nothing without enquiry and thought. We need to overcome our desire for the security of comfort, a ready acceptance of that which we don't feel we can change. If we evaluate a typical working day, we've already designed and operated multiple workarounds, easier and more reliable ways to get things done. It's pure instinct. We have to believe at all times that we can change anything for the better, that it's within our capabilities and our gift. A test of brokenness isn't required. And that if we can't change it ourselves, there will be others willing to do so with us. It just requires connection and exploration. We may feel as though we're alone at times, but we never are.

Chapter 9

"Teamwork makes the dream work"

But it doesn't. Does it?

Working together drives us. Almost no-one works alone. We search out others to make our ideas a reality. We've stressed the benefit of the collective on a number of occasions so far. It's beautifully captured in the oft-postered Ubuntu proverb, "I am because we are." Sometimes the ties between us in our work are strong, almost umbilical. Solid lines. Sometimes they're weak, dotted and even broken lines. The former has been chewed over by writers for decades. There's almost nothing left to say about relationships of magnitude, but somehow, we always manage to find more.

In regard to the latter, Mark Granovetter's seminal paper *The strength of weak ties* in 1973 credibly explored the latter in rather complex sociometric fashion.[89] Beyond academia, the essence of these micro-interactions was most poetically captured in the quite wonderful *Dictionary of Obscure Sorrows* by John Koenig (once a working website, now a holding page for a book awaiting publication) in the word "xeno" defined as: "The smallest measurable unit of human connection, typically exchanged between passing strangers—a flirtatious glance, a sympathetic nod, a shared laugh about some odd coincidence— moments that are fleeting and random but still contain powerful emotional nutrients that can alleviate the symptoms of feeling alone."

Even the most fleeting of moments between us is a reminder of our humanity, our shared consciousness. The passing of strangers is here envisaged in the corridor, the street, station, airport...or quite possibly now online. The emotional thud in the basement of our heart from the reading of a tweet that resonates, or a comment that strikes a recognizable chord. Not just a third level connection on LinkedIn.

Inevitably in the corporate world this gets translated into "teamwork" with all the intrinsic, arcane beauty unceremoniously whittled, so it fits on a slide deck. "You probably won't see this at the back." It's an emulsion brush for a filigree. Like most things of wonder the corporate world spits it out, tramples all over it, scoops it up and claims to have discovered something new and important. Let's see what we've got.

The unsettling phrase "only by working in a team will you fulfil your dreams" appears in the online marketing blurb[90] for a book by author John Maxwell, *Teamwork makes the dream work*. It's questionable in two respects. First, "a team." While we may not work solo, we may still not work in what might even remotely fit the definition of a team. It's quite possible simply to work with others as they and we need. Second, we may well achieve our "dreams" alone. They could be entirely individual affairs. We may need no-one's help at all beyond everyday commercial transactions. And a few xeno moments.

How many job adverts insist on being a "team player?" Barely any request the services of an anti-social loner, whose hobbies are bird watching and paintball gaming. Which is a true story, worryingly. Because we're a tad unnerved by those whose pursuits are entirely solo. Organizations want their people to work together. They see them as pieces of small jigsaws that are part of the overall big jigsaw, the box for which with the all-important picture on went in the recycling some years ago. They search for them, hope they'll slot into place, even like each other. They try and make sure they don't lose them by giving them good reason to stay. Rewards, benefits, apples. It explains the attachment – even obsession – in corporate life with the hegemony of the team. Yet we've never really mastered teams and teaming. Perhaps because we deploy the whole idea as though everyone gets it and few of those we consider participants really do.

What's in a team?

Many have tried to define what a team is, its fundamental characteristics.[91] In that kind of looking for things that aren't there kind of way that peppers management thinking and writing and saddles us all with having to try and read it. Yet it's fairly simple.

A team is two or more people working to a common, defined and agreed goal. Fundamentally it has to actually *be* a team for it to mean anything. Not just a clump with a label that suits someone, a convenience. Within the team a number of aspects may vary. The degree of formality. Is it part of the hierarchy, officially sanctioned, or a locally created unit unrecognized beyond its borders? The number of members. The roles of the members, the nature and quantity of their contribution, the time commitment and duration of stay of each. The exclusivity of each member – they may belong to more than one team. The team may or may not have a name, and its existence may be for any time period. All of which means "a team" requires a lot of clarification to be understood.

A team also has to *feel* like a team. With membership comes responsibility. That word again. Every member of a team is expected to make a contribution to the common goal. Yet even those teams with a clearly defined common goal may not witness such. The instinct of most organizations is to organize themselves in the manner of the hierarchical chart drawn by someone way down the slope and to define teams according to departments or practice groups. Regular, easy fare. It's a languid commonality to impose. In this sense, for an individual, membership of a team is given but participation isn't. We may be part of the Accounts Payable team and just do our own thing, following the given process, keeping our workarounds to our self, feeling no affinity with our colleagues or awareness that there's even a common goal beyond the day's workload or the lunchtime menu. We may speak to no-one. Weak ties only. We're essentially saying we're a group or collective rather than a team, but organizations rarely make that distinction. They call groups "teams" in the hope they may at some stage feel like a team, and so as not to relegate other collectives to a lesser status as that always leads to problems which lead to work. It's a non-differentiated label we're generally stuck with.

Finally, a team has to *behave* like a team. Not like a collection of individuals using the illusory cover of membership to pursue their own ends, shafting each other at every opportunity to ensure they attain them. Which means members have to want to be members and understand the requirements. Which means being loyal, trusting and oriented toward the common goal. Even if it means that personal ambitions suffer. There's an overly romanticized hope on the part of the instigators that in joining a team each member happily posts their own ambitions in a sealed box by the door. Not one made of an old cereal box. The threat of those aims being identified or suffocated by the team can often harden the resolve to pursue them at all costs.

In corporate life it's not like electing to join a sports team. Very often you just end up in a team. Placed. It might have a confused goal, be poorly led, suffer from internal conflict and offer no outlet for your views. Yet when you raise an issue beyond its confines, you're not being a team player. The only transfer you'll get is out.

However, in matters of teams it's almost impossible to escape the tiresome comparisons between corporate life and sport. Team identity and loyalty (complete with obligatory, if fleeting, badge kissing); playing to win; the balance between effort and skill; character and personality; the nuanced roles of managers, captains, coaches and players; plans, tactics and formations; awareness and the reading of the game; resilience, patience and determination; and specialists and generalists, to list a few.

Ideas of this nature always find their extremes, an example of which lies in the much-misinterpreted notion of the "corporate athlete," initially offered to the world in 1999 by Jack Groppel[92] and then taken up by Dr Jim Loehr and Tony Schwartz.[93] It's hard to imagine its thesis finding favor with the committed and talented yet utterly skint breaking their bodies week in week out for the rarest of shots at achieving the dream they've nurtured since infancy. The real athletes. Those engaged in the constant struggle for funding, whose families make huge financial sacrifices out of love and belief.

Especially when compared to the pampered, exceptionally rewarded captains of industry, whisked around in limousines, having to take a few tough decisions to justify the share awards. At the time of writing, a number of high-profile withdrawals from elite sports competitions on mental health grounds have highlighted the emotional as well as physical strain of such a life. Imagine for a moment, however, all those subscribing to the metaphor lined up for a grueling 3000m steeplechase in their normal daily attire for the chance to cross the line in the first three and keep their perks. A therapeutic daydream.

Fake teamery

There are numerous downsides of the organizational team obsession that drag members under the corporate surf with impunity and blow back on the originators with abandon.

First, they can quite successfully kill innovation. Underlying the idea of the team is the actual process of people working together. One of the most over-deployed and little understood words in the corporate vernacular is "collaboration," often used ubiquitously to refer to any form of working together. It's helpful to use the definition clarified by the Economist Intelligence Unit (EIU) in 2008[94] where a comparison is made with its two bedfellows, co-operation and co-ordination. All three are the stuff of teams, but the most precious and rare, collaboration, differs in that it necessitates an absence of compulsion. People freely decide to work together to create something new and of value. They think it's worthwhile and believe they can do it. Larry King was reputed to have called it "an unnatural act committed by consenting adults." Co-ordination, meanwhile, involves simply organizing with others to get something done that has to be done, and co-operation partaking with others in doing it. Both are centralizing forces – forms of control, input frameworks based on process – that create certainty and predictability.

In reality, the team is often a construct adept at enabling co-operation and co-ordination but an impediment to collaboration, which is more likely to occur between individuals from *different* teams or structures, or those floating between them. For the avoidance of any doubt, this doesn't happen at the mythical "watercooler," it's a much longer process principally comprising the progressive establishment of trust. It often arises in opposition to its environment rather than because of it, where it's perceived to be acting as a constraint. It contains a healthy germ of rebellion which in turn is often the quality it needs to come to life. Somewhere in collaboration is a desire for freedom, a clawing at the cloying corporate cobweb, a sense that the product of the time and thought invested will be the opportunity to leave the tedium and oppression of the present behind.

Second, they're often illusory. Despite the organizational drive to have people work in teams, we're still treated as individual carbon units. We're a person, we have personal details in the HR system, a staff number, and there's only one photo on our ID Card – our own. We come into the organization alone and exit alone. Like life. While our work massively depends on everyone in our team and those we interact with doing theirs properly, as theirs may depend on ours, we're set targets and appraised for what we specifically do (or don't) as if it can be separated, extracted. The irony being, of course, that the more a team player we are, as the advert required, the more difficult this extraction. Of course, this can work both ways. We can sparkle in a dreadful team or be dreadful in a sparkling team. Either way it merely reinforces the artificiality of the team.

Third, they're a much over-hyped panacea. Consequently, all sorts of assumptions get made about how teams should operate. The chemistry ripples into alchemy. Numbers of people, diversity of skills and perspectives, freedom or constraint to act and how they should be managed and led. As much depends on the goal and the context. Like most things. Why the team exists, what it's supposed to be doing, how it's supposed to be doing it, where it's doing it and where the effects will be felt. Yet very often philosophy leads where practicality would suffice. Which makes it generally unproductive and a crap experience for everyone concerned.

Google famously, at least for the duration of a *New York Times* article[95], tried with their "Project Aristotle" to understand the qualities of successful teams so they could replicate them. But they couldn't understand or replicate. After years of analysis, it simply boiled down to people being decent to, and trusting with, one another. Or, as the 30-year-old expression we referenced in Chapter 5 that still no-one outside a university can explain succinctly despite countless books and articles on it calls it, "psychological safety." Space for safe conflict, to think, feel and act without fear of judgment. At which, we're back to Bill and Ted again, and the thunderous simplicity of their wisdom.

Fourth, along with all the stuff that matters, teams suck up inordinate amounts of time in stuff that doesn't matter. They're industrial generators of noise. Here we cross the boundaries of other fundamental issues with corporate life, but they warrant consideration. That's because team membership comes with a visual and aural responsibility. The team is expected to demonstrate its value, often through the reinforcement of its existence and identity. This means drawing in the time of its members, as it's the sum of its parts. Which means dipping our hands into the usual tombola of excruciation in its service.

None is more galling than the burden of regular non-beneficial hub-and-spokes interaction, the "weekly team meeting." The ultimate exercise in just-in-case futility, principally to save the leader the faff of having to speak to everyone individually in that institutional fear of management we observed earlier. With this, on the part of each member comes the inevitable fine art of positioning. Judging when to speak or contribute. Wanting to be seen in a positive light, to emerge from the meeting at a higher standing than we entered. Which in turn attributes an arbitrary value to our meaningless participation. Another concentric circle in the eternal search for validation. The 2014 BBC television series *W1A* was particularly adept at identifying the personas we often encounter at the shiny table. Particularly those advertising their distance from any involvement in the onrushing calamity, thoughtfully offering their support to those who have been. Safely supportive, without consequence.

In this regard, at even moderately responsible levels and above we face the challenge of the yin and yang of time: management and maker.[96] We've become all too accustomed to the former and struggle to carve out the latter. Management time comes in neatly packaged half-hour blocks. We switch attention at the top and bottom of the hour as needed. Maker time is at least half an uninterrupted day in which to get entirely lost in creating something or solving problems. Even a half-hour dropped somewhere in the middle can kill the whole day stone dead, purely from an awareness of the existence of the interruption to come. It breaks the flow, not to be recovered. Even as members of a team we need maker time. We'll have things we have to do for the team, it's not just about being with the team. Even managers need maker time. As a maker may need a little management time. Yet maker time is a dwindling resource. Without it we're creatively anemic.

Fifth, there's the other overblown team activity – the social. The seemingly timeless value placed on those in a team being able to "let their hair down." Sexist idioms persist in this regard, regrettably, and all too often the insistence on the necessity for such occasions has a male origin. As such, nothing is able to strike fear in the soul quite like "we work hard but we play hard." As in, "we drink irresponsibly and are all on a written warning for the resulting behavior." Or worse, it's hushed up for the avoidance of negative publicity or the workload associated with having to do something about it and everyone is asked to say no more on the matter. While knowing a little more about someone's personal life because a half bottle of wine removed the inhibition that kept the information safely concealed may be considered beneficial, once revealed it doesn't return to whence it came. In the wrong hands it can be extremely dangerous, and the anxiety associated with its release highly corrosive.

For those who would consciously prefer to keep their working and personal lives separate – despite the horrifying idea (for all concerned) of bringing your "whole self" to work – a reluctance to share the enforced joy is often scorned. The guilty often prefer association. It can affect opportunities for career advancement and learning. Far from not "drinking with the right people," the gall of not drinking at all can be devastating.

Covid-19 gave birth to the "online social" where at least cool tea could pass for a 5 percent ABV beverage if required. The pulling of an inane face for the obligatory social media post of a team having a roaring time not talking about work while answering a few emails could say "dangerously irresponsible" from the comfort of the kitchen table. The safety glass of a monitor able to prevent the inevitable intrusion into personal space and a lifetime of embarrassment. Depending, of course, on what has been inadvertently left in camera shot behind the unsuspecting participant. We're all one careless oversight short of becoming a meme.

Sixth, there's the unfortunate, dewy-eyed and deluded tendency to conflate "team" with "family." The very idea of family conjures within us all a unique combination of extremes of joy and horror, often brought on through reflection on their shades of dysfunctionality. While we're thrown together with work colleagues, we have an opt-out. Similarly, we may be required to exercise the opt-out for one of our number. With families it's a heady mix of blood and contract that exacts a heavy price from a desire to step away. Families often have poor form, too, when it comes to diversity and inclusion, spread as they are across many generations of attitude and influence. It's an antiquated idea, the time for which passed many generations previous.

Then, finally, there's the rivalry. The intrusion of gamification into corporate life has its uses when deployed sparingly. Like most things. Ladders and league tables add to the tingle of sporting analogy. A bunch of people are going to "win" and probably brag. Another bunch of people are going to "lose" and likely feel crap or complain or cry foul. Most will remain in mid-table safety and not say much. Only the mature win with humility and lose with good grace – yet even the professionally competitive aren't especially accomplished at doing either. So, what chance do we have? The idea of competition being "healthy" appeals only to those who think they stand a chance of winning. For the rest, it just obscures the purpose of the day.

Un-f*cking the team

We reach for the team instinctively. There's no immediate downside in considering a team and teamwork. More people with the requisite skills, organized and clear in their task and mandate, intuitively feels more likely to be successful in solving a problem or creating something than an un-coordinated rabble.

The team is the immediately apparent signifier of community. The need for collective behavior and responsibility runs through the pages of this book. Yet the response is such that there are times when a team isn't suitable or needed, and instead becomes an incumbrance, or imbued with the potential to crush something precious with its mass, structure and protocols. There may also be a time where a team isn't enough, where the overlaps or even the spaces between them are more appropriate. And so our statement becomes:

"~~Teamwork makes the dream work~~"

"People, teams, organization: we know the time for each"

In this, the team remains a vital and proven vehicle. Just not for everything. So how do we un-fuck the team? There may be three places we can begin.

First, we evaluate whether the team is necessary for what's required. It's not a foregone conclusion. Where they are, we recognize the fact and do all we can to ensure they're both functional (they work) and a joy to be part of (we want to be there). That they achieve both isn't a foregone conclusion, either, just because we *call* them a team. It's quite possible to have one and not the other, so determination and commitment is needed to ensure both. Being a member of, especially leading, a team is an investment, not an accident or an inconvenience.

If things begin to go awry, we don't spend hours frantically flipping through back copies of our favorite business journal (admit it, you secretly have one) for insights into our supposed inadequacy or collect mounds of transient data that drowns us without insight, we resolve them together. Like grown-ups. Frailties and vulnerabilities and all. Immediately, not later. With honesty, openness and fairness, with the sole intent of putting the team back on track, restoring its factory settings.

And anyone actually uttering "psychological safety" in doing so collects and pays for the coffee while they reflect long and hard on too many lost hours on social platforms debating the finer meaning of something that should be a fundamental component of work, without exception.

All of which is, of course, so much more difficult than it sounds when relationships have deteriorated beyond the possibility of dialog, trust evaporated and with a looked-great-on-paper incurable arsehole or two in the mix. Sometimes the team has to shed to rebuild. That's not an admission of defeat on anyone's part, but a reflection of innate human diversity. Sometimes we just don't know until we start to work together. We may have at some time been that arsehole if we felt out of place, unwelcome, or struggled – the Roman poet Ovid was reputed to have mused: "Here I am barbarian for men understand me not." But we probably weren't before, or after.

Second, where teams aren't necessary, we don't force fit them. We don't assume they're the panacea, the only way in which to organize. It's not a failure or a chasm of competence to decide they're not necessary. We understand that we can work with others and get along extremely well without all the pseudo-sporting back-slapping high-fiving locker room camaraderie and the imposition of all those time and energy-sapping "things teams do."

Third, we have to make certain that we don't suffocate ideas beneath the team, its rituals and its expectations before they've become something tangible, possible. As we covered previously, we must create effective channels for ideas, from spark to execution. The team can be a place of nourishment, an environment in which the inspiration from an individual is turned into reality by the collective. While the team presents an opportunity, just as a formal project might be the least appropriate vehicle for an idea, the team might not be the body for nurture that it needs, either. As collaboration is often best enabled across teams than within them, we need to be honest about the existing team's capabilities and skills. It may require that at the right time a new team entirely is built around the idea, drawing people from their existing collectives or from outside altogether. Or that we're best to leave it with its creator to explore in the broader landscape until something makes sense and a time to act emerges. It's a complete anathema to the manner in which the corporate machine grinds, but better it lives outside it till it has form than is consumed by it. The team may come later. Or not at all. Whether we wear the badge or not, it's up to all of us to decide.

Chapter 10

"If we can't measure it, we can't manage it"

But we can. Can't we?

To say that Peter Drucker is revered as an organizational and management thinker rather underplays his legacy. Like saying Alan Turing dabbled with computers. He gave us "knowledge worker" and lots of us are just the thing, so we have an almost personal association. We see ourselves in his mirror. He's Pete. The trouble with being apotheosized is that you get held responsible for things you didn't say, too. Like any version of "if you can't measure it, you can't manage it." Also, not responsible, despite claims to the contrary, is the polymath W. Edwards Deming. He sounded a warning about important decisions being made based on measurement of the wrong things. But his caution was not born from the excruciating wasted time and needless anxiety associated with measuring stuff that no-one would ever be bothered with, or for the countless times it was used in the devious pursuit of advantage. Most management gurus sit in a lab. Or a temporary cabin in the car park. Not with the rest of us.

The regrettable phrase and the requisite tyranny it has bestowed contains two key terms – measurement and management. They're ripe for division and diminution.

First, measurement. Where quantitative, we set things into a common context using a device marked out in appropriate units. As they're standard, we all sign up to them. They mean something, because we can develop a shared sense of them. In isolation from the process of measuring, the units in the scale have an innate objectivity. That even applies where a qualitative scale such as percentages are used. The measures in turn feed our ability to estimate and develop shortcuts that ensure we don't freeze in apoplectic terror at not having the information needed to do anything. We can roughly know how far or fast something is, how heavy or hot. We trust ourselves. Naturally, therefore, measurement in many instances is beneficial, even essential. That it's not is far from the contention here, it's how measurement is used and that it's deemed to be an absolute requirement.

Then there's management. Where to begin? With control. It's all about containment, acting within. It exists in service of organizations that irrespective of sector or type are fundamentally designed to self-preserve, maximizing resilience through the minimum of effort or consumption of resources. As such management craves the core ingredients of control – data, certainty, resources and time. All the stuff of the world that's perpetually in short supply, yet that which feeds the cybernetic causal chain of acting, sensing and comparing against goals and then acting again. Where it can't find them, it has to improvise, whatever it takes. As such it's hard-wired to prevent things from happening. Or as it's called in the language beyond the revolving door, to "mitigate risk." Because risk is considered bad. When risk is realized, through a process of establishing the lowest common denominator, the most plausible junior person in the causal chain gets initially blamed (as we covered in Chapter 4) and if subsequently proved at fault probably disciplined, or worse, fired. In case it happens again and to encourage the others. The management machine therefore requires sating with measurement.

This isn't a startling revelation, of course. We just generally don't like to talk about it. We paint pictures of our organizations as dynamic, thrusting and fearless entities born in garages or telephone boxes with the disruptive impulse of a Nile perch. Even the scaliest, lumbering quadruped halfway to extinction is in someone's mind "just a big start-up, really." We're coming onto that in Chapter 12. There have been attempts to work with these tendencies and to balance the innate conservatism of organizations with the ever-changing environment in which they exist. The Viable System Model (VSM) of cybernetician Stafford Beer described in 1981 in *The Brain of the Firm*[97] attempted to balance the competing challenges of internal stability and adaptation. But the VSM relies on a highly complex dynamic fed by – yes, measurement. We're never far away.

This isn't a history book, but performance measurement goes back a long way. Luca Pacioli, the founder of modern accounting, stressed in his book *Summa de Arithmetica, Geometria. Proportioni et Proportionalita* (there are fewer snappier titles) in 1494 that business folk must have an orderly record of the performance of their operation. It sounds blindingly obvious today, but it began the development over the next several hundred years of performance measurement that eventually spawned generic instruments of everyday complexity such as balanced scorecards and performance matrices. Just as finding fault descends the internal corporate staircase in search of the lowest acceptable level to safely jettison, so does the responsibility for measurement.

From the late 1880s performance measurement really found its mojo with the birth of what became known as "scientific management" for its spawning of quantitative and mathematical methods. Referenced in Chapter 3, the individual whose focus on measuring the task efficiency of workers over time still generates the most emotion today when evaluating hard work is Frederick Winslow Taylor, stemming from his 1911 work *Scientific Management*.[98]

Shortly after publication the solidarity of the Taylorites was broken by the heresies of Frank Gilbreth and most notably Henry Gantt. The latter, he of the chart on every project manager's block, in particular saw the main cause of inefficiency not as the worker, but the *manager*. He elevated causality within the organization. It prompted efforts thereafter to consider a whole system approach reflecting the ever-increasing complexity of the environment in which organizations operated. Which at every stage has inevitably meant more measurement.

Quantifying the crap

There's a disorderly procession of problems with the opening proposition that will enable us to hammer it. Ten of them.

First, it's not easy. There are some fundamental issues with measurement that often mean what we consider to be true isn't. Not that they mean we shouldn't measure, of course. But it's not so simple. We can encounter any of these while remaining entirely unaware. We can do more than one at the same time. We could do all of them with deviously disguised incompetence. Here's a summary:

Inaccuracy: it's right enough (we think)

Bias: it feels right to me

Inconsistency: some of it's right

Distraction: it's interesting but not as much as THIS!

Timing: it looks right now

Accumulation: the stuff that's right is in there somewhere

Influence: they told us it was right

Invention: it may be right but who's to know?

Complexity: whatever it says it's probably right

Validation: we think it's right, but no-one checked

Second, so what? There's every possibility we've measured a lot of stuff for no reason at all. In actuality, every probability. Assuming we've overcome the challenges shown, do the measures mean anything? What are we going to specifically do with them? Will they inform a decision, an action or conscious inaction? Will they fuel anything positive at all? Can we even use them to actually manage anything? Most of the time, no.

Somewhere on the planet, visible from space, there's a mountain of measurement slowly stewing in its own unfulfilled promise. Or the promises we made for it. Because at some point we sought the time or investment necessary to gather the data, assuring those who signed the check that it would be worthwhile, that without it we couldn't manage.

Third, it's self-fulfilling. A job in itself. A distraction. Gathering measurements is relatively easy work. It is, in the main, compilation and aggregation. So, it's a useful distraction from doing anything challenging or beneficial – or risky. Assembling that monthly performance report against "Key Performance Indicators" (KPIs) is mindfully soporific and, of course, entirely necessary in the eyes of the person who won't bother reading it or doing anything with it but wants it *just in case*. KPIs are usually present because someone feels they ought to be. In themselves they may or may not be the right indicators, just indicators. Better to have some than none at all. Very often they bear no relation to the vision or objectives of the desired outcome. The other stuff, meanwhile, goes undone. Nobody got fired for compiling the regularly required stuff. And hardly anyone challenged its necessity as it also performs a periodic validatory role for the compiler. For whom else will do it if we don't? The mail must get through. The seasons turn, we compile the reports.

Fourth, it only tells part of the story. Usually because what's lacking is the story. Like a football team able to show a high percentage of possession, more shots on target and greater distance per player covered than their opponents while having been unceremoniously thrashed. With apologies for the sporting analogy. We can end up believing the measurement and not our own eyes or instincts. We become slaves to measurement and its outputs. Organizational examples are many. The time taken to complete something could be impressive but the actual output utter crap. We could have high attendance at events but those present could have been gauging themselves with the giveaway memory stick for the duration just to stave off unconsciousness, they just needed to show willing. We could collate impressive rates of satisfaction but those responding could have been entirely duped or are just happy to say anything, anything at all, so they can go home. Where the remainder of the story is missing, we make it up. We stitch together the measurements into a narrative that satisfies, complete with assumptions and interpretations. The measurements thereby inadvertently become "evidence." The circle of self-delusion is complete.

Fifth, it gets weaponized. All organizations are political. Strangely, everyone thinks theirs is more political than others. Politics is a sink hole. People and things vanish into it. Being political takes time and resources, which means that time and resource isn't being spent on something beneficial or useful to the organization. And the weapon of politics is measurement. It doesn't have to be fact. Just measurement. The ubiquity of misinformation in the global arena since the mid-2010s testifies to this. In 2017 the US President's aide Kellyanne Conway drew ridicule for her use of the term "alternative facts" to describe lies told by the Press Secretary of the time regarding the size of the President's inauguration crowd.[99] We've all seen the photos. She justified her approach on the basis that the crowd size could never be known. That is, where it's claimed that there's unlikely to be definitive measurement, making it up is fine. The danger arises when the measurements are used as (or by) an offensive tool. Their mere existence is the temptation. Which ensures that...

Sixth, it legitimizes fear as a management tool. Management by measurement means everyone somewhere at some time is on a graded scale for something. Sometimes we know where we are, sometimes we only know when we're told. It might be all of us, lock, stock and anxiety, or just a bit of us. The search for validation that generates the stress we referenced in Chapter 3 is about knowing where on that scale we are. It might be our measurements putting someone else's performance on a scale, even if we're not always aware of the implications. Yet measurement unlocks the potential to deploy fear. It's the beating black heart of every annual appraisal system, which we deal with in the next chapter, because let's face it, literally everyone hates them. We get told by someone who doesn't know the half of it what they've extrapolated to be the whole of it. For many, fear is power and it's directly proportional to their lack of ability. Because of this, it's rarely sustainable but the collateral damage can't always be undone.

Seventh, it magnifies disinterest. Sporadic measurement is often worse than none at all. As we referred to in Chapter 5, the Hawthorne effect revealed that when we're being watched, we tend to try harder. In *Smallcreep's Day* the workers felt that finally being paid some attention was beneficial: "It was so nice to feel that someone was taking an interest in us, we all worked harder, everyone in the factory."[100] That didn't last. Because it rarely lasts. The occasion of interest that's an annual appraisal often accentuates its paucity at all other times. It simply shows that a shit is only given when it absolutely has to be and only for as long as it needs to be.

Eighth, it stifles creativity. There are always too many accountants at every level of an organization. That's not a criticism, but a reality. They're needed within an organization. Just not so many of them. And accountants love and live for measurement. But they create a sense of safety, a comfort that risk is being mitigated. If we pair management with accounting, we perpetuate the most unimaginably self-reinforcing transactional caution, a literal chastity belt for innovation. A classic own goal, but one that appears to be the opposite because measurement – and the factors *being* measured – are woven into a story that tells us so. Pacioli's ghost haunts many a designated circulation route. No creativity, no innovation, no future. It's that simple a critical path. The outcome – exceptionally tightly run businesses heading for unaffectionate oblivion.

Ninth, it's culturally flawed. In some societies measurement is considered a negative pastime. "The standard Western management principle is 'If you can't measure it, you can't manage it.' In our ethos, 'if you measure it, you destroy it.'" So says Devdutt Pattanaik[101], renowned Indian mythology expert. He bases management practices on Hindu stories and rituals, a far more emotive approach than rational developed world doctrines. And he has a track record of success with his approach. We have a lot to learn.

Finally, the measurement might be accurate, objective and timely, but we're a crap manager. The opening expression of this chapter assumes innocently enough that measurement enables management. Maybe, just maybe, with all the key measurement data I could ever want, I couldn't hit a cow's arse with a banjo. Banjo dimensions, arse dimensions, wind speed, resistance, everything. People on hand to re-calibrate as I practice my swing. Footmarks on the floor and a precise tether for the unsuspecting bovine. But it's not to be, I miss, every time. Of course, it works both ways. As managers we measure, and as workers we're measured. We're often both subject and object. But either way, even excellent measurement guarantees nothing at all but the measurement.

Unmeasuring

Much of what's important in organizations can't be measured. In the pre-Covid days when it was quaintly thought necessary for administrative organizations to work almost exclusively in offices, most measures of success were input based: how much time we spent, when we were seen, when we were heard. What was more important than anything, was, we were there. Even if when we were there we were entirely useless. Or worse, made sure everyone with whom we came into contact was entirely useless by getting on their nerves all day. During the dark days we termed "lockdown," where we couldn't use our offices, there was celebration that we would be measured purely on our output, what we actually produced. But that was to fall foul of the equal and opposite tyranny of our value being determined by our inputs. We were ringing bells for the pre-schism Taylorites, for that was their mantra.

That's because so much of what we do that's of value can't be measured. Either quantitatively or qualitatively. We know it's of value because we can see the effects of our contribution. Sometimes a great deal later. On occasion, only when we're told. Things like mentoring, advice, support, encouragement, motivation, confidence, tentative first steps, relationships, trust and safety to name but a few. Take the last example. Just because there are zero lost hours reported from incidents and no records of near misses, doesn't mean the environment and practices are safe. It just means people may have been lucky and the admin associated with reporting a near miss so burdensome that no-one bothered. But we can contribute to a safe environment by taking responsibility, knowing what's needed, testing what appears uncertain, reporting what's needed and doing everything possible to improve what we can. All of us.

All the features listed are the stuff of human development, motivation, satisfaction and creativity. The stuff that's likely to be important, interesting, challenging and tangential. For which people make an effort because they want to. That makes everyone feel good about work and valued at work. That fires the present and future.

The un-measurable stuff still needs management. But a management that sets it free rather than constrains it. That allows it to flourish. That uses uniquely human skills. Like judgment, empathy, intuition, emotion and connection. As author (and like-loather of the adage heading this chapter) Liz Ryan remarks: "Luckily, humans are very good at reading energy and responding to it."[102] It's a poetic idea. Applying a measurement-based management style to these features of our working life is sure as heck going to squeeze the life out of them. So, what can't be measured can't be managed *as though it were being measured*. Or it will die. We'll only notice it when it's not here anymore. And no-one else is here anymore.

Un-f✳cking measurement

As glaring a target as the opening statement offers, it's still uttered with impunity. Of course, it's once again a question of balance. Some things need measuring, and some don't. It's about applying ourselves to determine the right ones in each case. Some things need managing and some don't. The same principle applies. Yet that doesn't mean ignoring those things it's decided don't warrant measurement or management. They may just be the most important aspects of our working lives. The attention they need is guidance. Our statement therefore becomes:

"~~If we can't measure it, we can't manage it~~"

"We measure and manage what we need – and guide the rest"

Naturally this is much tougher for those who are in a position of management. They have to decide. And they could get it wrong. The temptation to preventively carpet bomb every scenario is ever-present, as are, of course, the consequences as we intimated above: there won't be anyone around to measure or manage.

So how do we un-fuck measurement? Three possible places to begin are as follows.

First, we define its purpose. We understand why we need to measure something, how we do so and what it is – and develop the means to simultaneously measure and validate. There's a natural sequence, a critical path if we will. The why stems from asking the right question. The responses "because it's been requested" or "it's needed by management" aren't valid. Where we're the instigator it necessitates awareness. Where we're the recipient of a request (read, instruction), it can place us in an awkward position. That's a call we need to make – whether to challenge, and if so, how. If we can satisfy the why and can't answer the how, the same outcome. Finally, we need to be clear on what it is we need. We understand that incorrect measurement can wreak vastly disproportionate damage if not recognized for what it is.

Second, we're sparing with it. We avoid the temptation to try and measure what can't be, or doesn't need to be, in the deluded belief it's essential. We understand that measurement of itself doesn't make us a better manager. A huge swathe of the natural habitat of the corporate and organizational lies outside of measurable reach, where it's essential that it's allowed to flourish. It's the environment in which management ability is truly tested. It then makes the things we measure, when we're confident they're necessary and right, more meaningful and more likely to be respected and taken seriously. We value it, rather than feel our shoulders droop and our spirit wilt at the mere thought.

Third, we're careful with its use. Very often we're unsure who is guarding the guards. The misuse of measurement within an organization is often one stage removed from ourselves, by those who've not been involved in the process above but are merely presented with the opportunity. We therefore understand and define the ground rules for handling measurement when we have it. Who uses it (and how far it travels), what for and why – and how we respond in such circumstances if we don't have measurement where it's expected we should. We don't leave it lying around or distribute it freely. It's another level of interrogation, but an essential one.

And in doing all of this, we set ourselves free.

Chapter 11

"People are our greatest asset"

But we're not. Are we?

An asset is a thing or person that has use or value that's likely to put us at an advantage. A liability is a thing or person likely to put us at a disadvantage. Every organization would place its people in one or the other column, despite claiming they were all assets. The statement therefore actually means: "Some of our people are assets. The others aren't." Sometimes it can be surprising that a liability becomes an asset before they're fired, or that an asset in whom time and money was invested becomes a liability. Some businesses have assets that are far more valuable than their people – industries such as manufacturing and extraction, for example. And every organization drains the last drop of expertise out of its people to make its systems and processes resilient to the loss of its people. That is, it makes sure that their people aren't their greatest asset, but their creations are.

"People assets" are rarely tied into the organization long term, unless they're at a very senior level, unlike those for which capital has been expended. The commitment is often the length of a formal notice period, unless a "technicality" can be found to hasten the process where it goes sour. Organizations struggle continually with the conflicting demands of retention and refreshment. The adage of unknown origin: "Suppose we train our people and they leave? Suppose we don't and they stay?" captures it succinctly. Long Term Incentive Plans (LTIPs) and Retention Bonuses are often deployed, but they can backfire. We're all lumped into a statistic known as "turnover" – how many join, how many leave. Irrespective of whether the right people joined or left. It's the sort of data that cools the heart – as we covered in Chapter 10.

We can't forget that organizations are essentially a composite of their people. While there are increasingly automated processes that spin without intervention, humans created them. Yet they're personified as though they had an individual mind and a will, the ability to determine strategy and take decisions, independent of their constituent parts. Emotions, even. A legal entity they may be, with ownership of varying types, but if everyone got up from their chair and left they would be but a husk.

The world of employment has changed dramatically in the decade prior to the time of writing too. "Our people" would previously mean simply employees. Yet the associations with the mission and purpose of the organization can now take on a whole spectrum of possibilities on fixed or variable terms. Economist Li Jin argues that work is being "unbundled" from employment[103] creating a new cohort of "micro-entrepreneurs" where once William Whyte's dutiful and faithful "organization man" toiled, comfortably subsumed.[104] The rise of the freelance "gig" or "sharing" economy – comprising discrete tasks performed for organizations as required by self-employed workers, arranged via platforms of exchange – has reduced the reliance on the part of many employers on those under formal evergreen contracts. By the end of 2019, fully 5 million people were self-employed in the UK – 15 percent of the workforce. Not all such were from choice. Many of those unable to find full-time work have felt compelled to set themselves up as a visible operation so as not to appear unemployed. Who therefore are "our" people now?

While the successful minority of freelancers proudly wave their flag of liberty – "I've got a hundred problems but a boss isn't one of them" – for all the negatives, employment within a stable organization offers safety and security not found outside.

This usually includes benefits beyond salary that freelancers rarely bother to fund themselves – like private healthcare, so if you break you can get patched up and back to your station more quickly. And sick pay while you're being patched.

Assets, particularly of the carbon form, need acquiring, managing and developing. We'll deal with acquisition in Chapter 13 when we look at the workplace experience. Here we'll focus on the managing and developing.

Management

Of course, many would say, management is *the* problem. The source of all workplace ills and frustrations, organizational permafrost. The comedian Alexi Sayle captured this common spirit of contempt when on his show *Stuff* (1988-91) he asked: "Think about your boss for a moment...go on...aren't they a complete *twat*?" Yet when the laughter died down, we realized the joke was on us too. Many of us are in some way both manager and managed, villain and victim, irrespective of the organizational structure we covered in Chapter 4. Conflicted.

On the business bookshelves, in the procession of tracts awaiting merciful pulping, managers come off far worse than leaders, even though to a degree every manager is a leader and every leader a manager. Leaders make things happen, galvanize, inspire, motivate, transform, empower. They get shit done. We willingly follow them over the cliff. When it's bad shit they get done, it's to a grisly end.

Protest as we may at the apparent dearth of quality or integrity, we've collectively made management the problem. It doesn't have to be so. We've no doubt all heard of the "Peter Principle" – named after its creator, Laurence Peter – whereby we're promoted to our level of incompetence.[105] We've also seen too many talented specialists sprung out of their professional love affair into responsible roles they loathe. Somewhere in the organizational shakedown someone's making these decisions, they don't happen on their own. Probably those for which either of the above has happened. They have a knack of self-perpetuation.

It means for many managers and their unfortunate HR departments that the oft-taken path in difficult situations is a swift team re-organization, re-adjustment of roles and a redundancy or two. It may prompt a small spike in the demand on time but it's a lot less overall than actually bothering to invest in managing someone effectively such that the situation could have been avoided. And so, without evidence the situation moves to a compromise agreement and a pay-off, a loss of confidence and reputation on the part of the exited individual, and a swift kick in the soft tissue of the organization's reputation.

Of course, a small number of managers slip through the net, those for whom it's a vocation. We've all probably recognized the beneficial contribution that a fantastic manager has made to a role we've held, or to our career. As though it were something of a miracle, a remarkable exception. We call them out for their excellence because of the sea of mediocrity from which they're plucked. "They do exist, I've known one!" It's entirely the reverse of the situation we *should* encounter.

Where we try and give managers the competence they need, we often respond with just what's not required, the one-size-fits no-one "management development program." Why we would consider that management is about understanding people's individual needs and tailoring our approach to enable them to be the best they can be to then put our aspiring cohort through an economy sausage machine beggars belief. It's no surprise that what emerges are identically ill-equipped economy sausages. It's a marked failure of the development we'll shortly cover, working its way back into our ability to look after our greatest asset.

Yet in the modern world of work, stardom beckons. Everyone wants to be the high-earning, freewheeling, unorthodox maverick. Or the new gilt-edged, spangled superstar, the "founder." Even if what's been founded is crap. It's a symptom of the atomization of work referenced in Chapter 2, the descent into individualism. In this respect, management is no longer aspirational, if it ever was. We want to be responsible for just *us*, not others. Managers have become the ultimate un-valued asset. We've made it the poisoned chalice – the role we don't want, that we gift to those to whom we wish to attach a rusty ball and chain. If we do accidentally find ourselves within, having misjudged the situation, we live with the expectation that when the inevitable cyclical cull begins, we'll be one of the first. We've become fearful of it. Because everyone thinks we're unnecessary. We're the ones controlling, preventing, obfuscating, perpetually getting in the way, the visible bidders of the organization's desire to conserve and contain. So, we're the target.

As a manager, we find that we've no time for our "own job" because looking after our people voraciously consumes it all, even though that's what we're supposed to be doing. It *is* our job. As we get drawn into difficult situations and circumstances, we don't see that those needing attention are often high potential individuals, lost and frustrated, who require the benefit of our guidance. We begin instead to value those who are, as we describe them, "low maintenance," who don't appear to need any supervision or mentoring as they seem to be just fine. So, we don't give them any, when they need it too. So, we screw it up both ways. No-one is being served well by the arrangement. So, what we find is it's crap being a manager and it's crap being managed.

Development

Development comes in three key forms – in the role itself, either by discovery, instruction or what's been termed "osmosis" (observing others); through mentoring and guidance by a line manager or colleague; or formal training. It has become common practice to assume that the percentage of each is roughly 70:20:10. The effort and expense required for each in reverse order. It's especially useful for an organization as they can effectively duck 90 percent of the responsibility and expect that managers – yes, them again – can handle it. Of course, it's not a blame culture, but if potential isn't realized, there's only one point of responsibility and that's the individual concerned.

This isn't to be confused with an approach pioneered by the former CEO and Chairman of General Electric, Jack Welch, termed the "vitality curve," a name that dressed pure corporate ruthlessness in the guise of a wellbeing program. "Rank and yank" as it was nicknamed held that at any time 20 percent of "people assets" were over-performing, 70 percent were bang average while the bottom 10 percent needed to be exited regardless of the circumstances. Of course, it's roots lay in an idea dating back to the fifth century BCE where in cases of cowardice or desertion Roman legions were decimated – one in ten men being executed, often selected through the drawing of lots, as a motivation to the others to try harder. While it was acknowledged that some people regrettably slipped into the wrong bucket, particularly the exit bucket, the vitality curve was so deemed to work that it was frequently copied. Despite claims that it generated substantial earnings growth, the system couldn't be proven to be the sole attributed cause. GE dropped it in 2015. We ought to be aware that variants are still out there under assumed identities, hiding in plain sight.

In most organizations, development is formally documented in the most rudimentary and detested of all standardized processes to which we hinted in the last chapter, the individual annual performance review or appraisal. No-one likes giving them, no-one likes receiving them. Yet they persist. Our entire year's effort is reduced to an evidence-scant subjective assessment, sometimes aggregated into a score – alpha or numeric – that affects progress, bonus, remuneration, opportunity and our sense of justice and self-worth. We clench every orifice in our body, even those we didn't know we could (or had), as we listen to someone else's views on how we've performed. Someone who wasn't there, didn't feel what we felt, didn't see how others enabled or prevented us doing what we could have. It's always stated that the annual appraisal should contain no surprises, but that assumes anyone's paid attention to our work during the year. Even those accused of micromanagement or any of the forms of monitoring we covered in Chapter 5. So, they invariably do.

They're dressed in the finery of the opportunity to guide the recipient. To see what's required from the 70, 20 and 10. To determine what resources are needed. It's a bold move to reverse the appraisal: "How am I doing as a manager? What do you need from me?" It's difficult, without fear of consequences, to respond with more time, more interest, a more consistent attitude, less arbitrary decision-making, a greater degree of fairness, mentoring, an understanding of my personal constraints and the battles I'm fighting, and perhaps a touch of empathy, without it turning sour. "Yes, sorry to have to tell you, but you're a duff boss. Can I have a new one?"

What are the alternatives? As with everything that involves a periodic intervention, the alternative lies in the continual, smaller-scale investment in time and energy. The spirit, if not the practice, of the Agile process. From weekly or fortnightly check-ins (what we've come to term "1:1"s), end-of-project reviews or simply breaking down the annual review into a dozen bite-sized chunks. That involves a far greater commitment of time and interest on the part of both parties. We could, of course, install one of those feedback devices found in airport toilets and each push the red, amber or green button every time we finish a catch-up.[106] It's a data-gathering technique that's proven remarkably insightful. It could change the course of management and development for all time.

Most organizations rarely signal their development interest and intent. Their physical spaces for the purpose often reside in the darkest corners of their workplace or in the basement, if they have any at all in which case, they're reduced to squatting wherever possible. They rarely seem to understand that actually investing in such spaces and ensuring they're prominent, even front and center, signals an irresistible intent. Even if many people don't attend them, they see them and recognize the value attached. It drives learning interest and behavior. Yet the ubiquitous and often anecdotal claims (even when data from a booking system exists to prove the contrary) that there "aren't enough meeting rooms" prevails and the flexible, learning-friendly furniture and technology makes way for a lacquered table and an oil on canvas.

Recognition

In terms of the day-to-day, the asset-boosters, the rocket fuel of corporate and industrial life, are thanks and recognition. Thanks, because, as we've explored, it's vital that we feel our work matters. Recognition because, over and above what we're expected to do, we've been seen and acknowledged to have gone further. That might be as a one-off or over a period of time. We'll have and enjoy the dopamine shot and it'll have us trying for another. Most of the time it involves nothing but human behavior, which may suggest it's easy and free but inevitably means it's often scarce and needing of a formal scheme to ensure it happens at all. But absolutely vital they both are.

Where things aren't going as well as to warrant thanks or recognition, asking for help in regard to either the volume or difficulty of the challenge remains problematic for most. We believe somehow we'll be considered less capable, and thereby disadvantaged. So, we look for other sources of help – friends, peers, our team. Or YouTube, naturally. We may rely on managers to detect its necessity and raise it for us, in fulfilling their "pastoral" role (originally meant as spiritual guidance but now used to refer to anything related to care). Such an intervention may still be brushed away in fear of the same outcome. Stories help. Particularly where it's the manager telling the story of how they asked for help, the signal of vulnerability that says asking is okay: "I did; you can, too."

Knowledge

The handy thing about our people assets, particularly when they're developed, is that they create other assets, primarily in the form of knowledge. It may be as plans, ideas (as we covered in Chapter 8), markets, inventions, processes, networks, how to get things done, or the hidden paths. Yet almost every organization struggles with its sharing and availability, and willingly lets that knowledge and expertise walk out of the door with its creator. It's usually more expensive and time consuming to buy it again from elsewhere, or re-create it, than to keep it.

At a certain point in the relationship between the individual and the organization, it becomes apparent it has no future, whosoever determines it. Thereafter, the former begins to detach themselves and their stuff from the latter. The fabled "handover" is rarely more than cursory. On arrival in a new role, we spend a considerable amount of time and focus searching for and re-building the knowledge required to be able to do our job. At scale, it creates a perpetual overlap, a repetition of tasks, like the ebb and flow of the tide.

Opportunity

With management and development comes opportunity. It's pointless identifying the right people, taking exceptional care of them and developing their skills, abilities and knowledge, helping them create networks that ensure they can navigate the complexities of the organization, to then block all roads from this point onwards. Consciously or unconsciously. We considered the need to provide opportunity from the equality perspective in Chapter 6.

Organizations rely extensively on a great many of their people not being particularly ambitious, either in regard to navigating the hierarchy or broadening their knowledge and skills. They wouldn't be able to cope with such a seething mass of desire. It involves ensuring that it isn't inadvertently stimulated, just in case. If the arrangement suits both parties, there's nothing wrong with its perpetuation.

For those, however, who do wish to progress, there's a simple outcome from a lack of opportunity – exit. If momentum cannot find a pathway within, it will source another. Sometimes that momentum is displayed or is obvious, other times it's hidden, only revealed as the access pass is returned. In the latter case it reveals a lack of care and interest in the individual, justifying their decision. Having nowhere to go is the most pressing point of tension and frustration in many organizations. Waiting for that elusive shard of light can be torture. Opportunity can't be an afterthought.

We may think we've covered all there is to say about looking after our people. But then, after surviving it all, navigating every arbitrary and institutional hurdle, comes the memo: our role is being transferred to Düsseldorf at the end of the month. We can go, or we can *go*. Choice. Wonderful, isn't it?

Asset stripping

There are a number of reasons why the claim to the importance attached to people within organizations can be so damaging.

First, the often arbitrary and subjective nature of management and development can erode a belief in fairness and objectivity within the organization. Without clear, evident and re-told examples to the contrary, acknowledgment, recognition, reward and opportunity can appear to bear no relation to innovation, effort or achievement. The prevailing understanding emerges that the only way to a sustainable career is through "managing upwards" as it's technically referred to, "sucking up" as it's more commonly known. That is, preserving excellent relations with those more senior by being ultra-visible, responding to requests with urgency and flattering where every opening invites. And, of course, not questioning, challenging or speaking out of turn. We all at some point become caught in its cloying dishonesty.

Second, the locus of responsibility for people can be unclear, and becomes chased through the organization like Pacman. It reflects a lack of respect for the vital role of management as a discipline and vocation. While the mantra is echoed, its application defies practicality. The organization expects its managers to take the lead, to bear the bulk of the responsibility; its managers meanwhile look to its systems, schemes and programs to deliver, and rue that those they're required to manage lack the competence and experience required. Leaders task their charges with managing teams while loading them with responsibilities that deny them the time required to manage.

Third, most of the benefit to ourselves comes from our own personal investment in learning and development, not that offered by the organization. The corporate cop-out that's "self-directed learning." As in, if you want to know something, find out for yourself because you'll wait an age for anyone here to help you. That includes network creation and the search for suitable mentors, both within and externally. It's fortunately become commonplace in the absence of anything approaching functional in most organizations to simply ask – "will you mentor me?" Most of those identified by the seeker to be worthy of providing mentoring are decent enough to accept and even flattered by the invitation. If we're asked, we're often delighted, amid the chaos, to be able to give something back.

Fourth, we're all too damn busy. Whether we're busy with anything meaningful, or handling a workload that's reasonable, is questioned elsewhere in this book – but overloaded, nonetheless. Too busy to manage, too busy to be managed. Too busy to manage in that we avoid doing anything more than we have to because it's our work that the grinding system of appraisal observes and ranks in a system that's incapable of recognizing how to identify that we've been able to help people be the best they can be. It's about tangible, measurable results. Management is just something we do because it's the level we're at. Too busy to be managed in that we avoid interaction unless we have to, we duck under the radar in fear of being asked to do more because we already can't do what we have in front of us. So, we're all in perpetual avoidance mode. The alternatives appear terrifying – more meetings, more records, more planning, more listening, more thinking. The mechanics of the organization require management to be effective in order for it to function and grow, and for its people to flourish, yet inadvertently do everything possible to prevent it being so. We step outside its reach in both respects out of pure self-preservation.

Un-f✳cking mismanagement

"People centricity" is an undeniable aim in so many aspects of organizational life. Who couldn't wish to put people first in everything? While entirely noble it's constantly at odds with the perpetuating need for members of the organization to ensure it *survives* its people. In each case enough individuals are driven to think and act as though, while others may drift away, they will remain. How long doesn't matter, it appears as though forever from where we stand. For people centricity therefore read expediency. Whatever it takes. And so, our statement needs to reflect our inclusion, and that of both the individual and collective interest:

"~~People are our greatest asset~~"

"We are our organization"

It unifies rather than divides. It removes the sense that some are controlling, others controlled, the divide between "us and them." It implies equality through association, and a genuine sense of opportunity and mobility should it be desired.

So how do we un-fuck the mismanagement – possibly even non-management – of the organization? There are three ways we can begin.

First, we need to rebuild the value of management, understanding why we need it, how it should be done and what it entails. That is, managing and being managed. It's the enabler of the development, learning and growth of everyone within the organization. Which means the systems and processes of the organization must be geared toward each and be able to recognize its excellence. In doing so we can make management aspirational, a valued necessity, a people-centric activity. Something we strive to do, and do well. Not in the administration of things, but in the care of, and respect for, our colleagues. In doing so, we ensure that we create a seamless path between joining an organization, being cared for and managed, developed and motivated, and offered opportunity. The unfortunate pervading story of management – as an unnecessary encumbrance, as a block to progress, fixated on control – has to become one of enablement and liberation. It means management going against the grain of the organization itself. Which requires investment and energy. It's a two-way process, we need to value being managed too – but we can when we sense interest, fairness and commitment. They're all equally important and create the essential, holistic experience of work. We may not all be ambitious, which is fine too – our needs may not be lesser, just different. But needs, nonetheless.

That's not to deny there will be times where control must be exercised, difficult conversations had and unpalatable decisions made. It's not an unrealistic, misty-eyed vision of permissiveness. But they'll no longer be the *raison d'être*. We can, although we seldom like to admit it, sometimes be glad of being reined in, our exuberance curbed where we perhaps haven't thought something through or have been caught up in an idea that has taken on a life of its own. Control and care needn't be counterparts.

Second, we must stop considering people as an "asset," as something on a register, immobile, deteriorating but for preventive and reactive maintenance. It's the same grim territory as being a "resource" or worse still, being regarded as "human capital." It confuses talented, emotional and vulnerable individuals with the inanimate, fixed life, static means to production. The term perpetuates our fixation with output and productivity – results – and is unable to comprehend and process the wider contribution we make to our organization, and its broader circles of similarly fragile yet exceptional beings. Humans need to be referred to in human terms, not those of the balance sheet or ledger. Our people are our greatest contributors.

Finally, we cease referring to "people" as though we're not one of them. We acknowledge the fact that the organization is nothing without everyone within it. We recognize the place of teams and other forms of association within, as they're needed and as they evolve and change. Which means we're involved, complicit, conflicted – and therefore able to influence and create change. Whatever its structure, wherever we reside, whatever our ambitions. With the tweak of a few words, it's suddenly empowering. Words matter. What we do, though, matters more. In this way we'll see and know that our organization values us, and in turn we'll value it and everyone that comprises it.

We succeed or fail together.

Chapter 12

"We're like a big start-up"

But we're not. Are we?

Stardom has many pathways, many outcomes. It's hard to watch TV programs like *The Apprentice* and think that rock and roll and business have anything in common. Something feels instinctively wrong when those in their early twenties seem to have more interest in developing a marketing plan for lichen cheese than trying to remember where they left their shoes after the open jam session at the Duck's Head on Half Price Monday. The common strand of DNA is the emotional wrecking ball that is hype. And the rapid pursuit of wealth, of course.

We've all had a killer business idea at some point in our lives. We've let it slip away because we didn't have the stomach or resilience or self-belief or friends with cash under the floorboards to be an entrepreneur. We've all then seen "that" idea at some later point morph into a successful service or product and thrust its originator into a world of Sunday supplement interviews and posts about why getting up at 4am and drinking hyper-condensed kale juice is a key to their success. We've told our network that we thought of it first and idly pondered the "if only" of life in the spotlight before getting back to our spreadsheet and unreasonable deadline.

All businesses had to "start-up" at some point – every dinosaur began life in an egg. Yet the internet did two related things to change, literally, everything: it reduced logistical and financial barriers to entry for a new business (to get in), and it enabled the business to scale rapidly (to get big) – with the right management, risk-taking, investment and good fortune, naturally – through being able to almost simultaneously surface an idea and make it happen. Or at least a minimum viable version of it. Often even a crap version of it if the idea held enough potential to shake things up in a stale and predictable market locked in a stranglehold by archaic, crusty organizations. All without having to bother with either profitability or the capital-intensive millstones of their forebears.

Start-ups became associated with a cocktail of ideas and behavior that were deemed "disruptive," a term coined by Clayton Christensen and friends in the mid-1990s. To established industry a negative term, yet one that epitomized the excitement, danger, optimism, spirit and impatience of the upstarts. They promised newer, better and lower cost life-transforming stuff. Consumers loved them. With the expectation of geometric returns in almost imperceptible timeframes, venture capitalists loved them, too. It meant doing things differently in every respect, not so much new rules as no rules.

The first coming was the dot-com bubble of the late 1990s/early 2000s where the promise – rather than the reality – of internet-powered business led to the ridiculous over-inflation of the value of many new enterprises. It originally centered on "Silicon Valley" in California, in the area around Stanford University. The geographic term was first used[107] in 1971 in the magazine *Electronic News* to refer to companies manufacturing semiconductors. While some of today's giants were spawned in this locale, almost every country today claims an area hosting a vibrant "start-up scene," albeit usually as a means of boosting corporate property letting to kick-start urban regeneration.

The dot-com bubble burst, of course, and a lot of people lost a lot of money and were rather embarrassed at having been caught up in the almost apoplectic investment frenzy. A few start-ups survived the carnage and prospered to become the digital leviathans of today, and a great number of ideas that didn't find commercial success at the time have emerged since with more confidence, opportunity and technical know-how. Start-up learned its lessons.

We should always remember that, like bands and artists, even today most start-ups don't commercially succeed. The failure figure in 2019[108] in the US was around 90 percent. The music industry pre-streaming would anecdotally assume that only one in ten artists would repay their initial advance. As with start-ups, those that did usually did so handsomely. Luke Haines, founder of the band The Auteurs, stated in his autobiographical book *Bad Vibes*: "Musicians like to see themselves as outsiders and outlaws. The trouble is most outsiders are not that successful."[109] That still doesn't stop anyone trying. Or pretending.

It's often why the oldest, stalest farts in the commercial world like to think of themselves as start-ups. It's got nothing to do with innovative brilliance, or the courage and tenacity to scale oxygen-starved commercial heights while teetering on the brink of the abyss. It has everything to do with the associated behavior – the manufacturing of a twinkle in the eye, hint of trouble, smell of teen spirit, air of slightly insane unpredictability that makes us want to head off on a voyage of discovery of our darkest, innermost self. A second coming for the dream of rock and roll immortality. It ignores the fact that it's a public limited company that's spent the last few decades wondering why its declared aim of "increasing shareholder value" hasn't especially resonated with its people such that the most talented of them have left and that the disruptors have taken half their market while they've been deciding which hoodie to wear.

That's because for the universally fucked world of work the very idea of "start-up" – even aside from the actuality – is a clear and present danger when in the hands of anyone who isn't running a start-up but thinks they are. It thereafter duly dumps on us all as the operation of the organization becomes infused with the fantasy.

Start-up self-delusion

So, what damage does the aberration of being "a big start-up" in the mind of a leader wreak?

First, it's a bully's backstage pass. The challenge and stress of running a start-up is beyond the comprehension of almost every payrolled employee. It's why so few attempt it. The start-up scene is filtered for our sanitized consumption. We only hear about success, failure isn't a story unless there's a scandal associated. The airbrushed hype ignores the human toll in pursuit of unfeasibly rapid success. And so, from within the protective corporate shell breaks a delusion that spawns a catalog of behavior that has no place anywhere in the world of work. Not even in a start-up.

It's the sense that decisions must be made immediately, and action follow instantaneously. Consequences can be untangled later, if we haven't all moved on to the next imbroglio before then. That human feelings have no place in the pursuit of rewards when time is the ultimate driver. That process is a mere obstacle, analysis the penultimate breath of extinction. It's the living embodiment of "JFDI," with the insertion of the obscenity (willfully used in this book, it has to be said) into the Nike slogan[110] of 1988: "Just do it." It was rather lugubriously prompted by the last words of the convicted criminal Gary Gilmore in 1977 as he faced a firing squad in Utah, who demanded of his executioners "let's do it." An eternal darkness lurking within a mere few words. Yet what feels like action-oriented spontaneity, riding the white horses of opportunity, is in effect a regrettably conscious decision not to do anything expected and to hell with the effects.

When this veil of artificial urgency is drawn in a corporate environment in which time's significance is illusory, "command and control" finds new voice. Alternative views are rejected. Dissent of even the most interested and caring form is void. All that matters is that stuff gets done. Even if it's the wrong stuff.

The pressure becomes magnified, it rebounds and reverberates. Unlike in a small start-up it's clear where it begins and ends, but not so in a larger organization. Yet no matter the stress, if you're employing and managing people, there's never a justification. If you feel you have to – worse still, have a right to – behave this way, it's time to give it up. The guitar is probably still in the loft.

We then have myth. The start-up scene is also a seething, bubbling, fermenting pool of quasi-religious flannel. Probably more cult than religion. Unfortunately, that is, flannel that's so incredibly easy to be seduced by until it solidifies into belief. It feeds the oppression. Its power is that it positively shimmers with originality and difference. "Start-up is a state of mind," said one CEO.[111] It implies that in partaking we're both signing up to something new (that we don't understand) and leaving previously held views at the door (that underpinned the cultures of the organization). The stuff that gets talked about doesn't sound like work. It smacks of freedom. They have places to work, too, that feed the myth. WeWork, as a brand defining the genre, shattered the dull, sewn-up world of real estate in a relative nano-second by creating environments resembling more a youth club or university common room, symbolized by the perk that no-one asked for, the beer tap. Most corporates had banned drinking in working hours many years prior. Start-up has beer.

Together the myth and oppression begin to create an air of invincibility. Like a start-up whose coffers have just been stuffed with saffron by an angel investor, prompting a rash of spending on all the wrong things, a sense emerges that whatever happens nothing bad will happen. That courage is its own reward. That the organization is blessed. Start-up is full of mantras like the claim that doing what you love will bring rewards, and that failure withers in the face of unrelenting persistence. Neither, of course, is true. What you love might be a crap idea and to keep going will just burn cash faster than KLF with a briefcase.[112] No business is invincible, especially one that believes itself to be. And even more specially one that believes itself to be because it thinks it's something else entirely. Business is jobs, livelihoods, families, education, opportunity, learning, growth, dignity. It's trivialization benefits no-one. The reality is, when disaster strikes most of those on the "shop floor" have seen and heard it coming for some time but have been powerless to stop it.

Finally, it breeds amateurism. At this juncture there's a conflict. Some sluggish, tedious, uninspiring and protectionist markets have been ripe for disruption for decades. Start-ups therein have benefited consumers enormously, forcing surviving operators to slash prices, and improve their range and quality of service and customer orientation. Many such aren't from the sector, but outsiders. Business folk with an ability to sense an opening. Like the founders of Uber setting up after struggling to hail a taxi in Paris. The amateur operates at the heart of collaborative consumption. Yet the world has, in the last 2010s, had a bellyful of dissing experts and the political and social carnage it has wrought.

Careers are built on harnessing knowledge and experience. The notion of "hiring for attitude and teaching the rest" still implies a need for knowing what to do and getting better at it with time, even if not immediately. Even the idea of "serial incompetence" – mastering a skill then starting to learn a new one afresh – suggests an aptitude for acquisition, a grounding to work on. Yet the notion of just needing energy and spirit to succeed is often entirely misplaced.

Back to the rock and roll parallels. Punk rock, emerging in the US in 1975 and the UK a year later, brought together adrenaline junkies who initially weren't sure which way around to hold a guitar with those who had been learning and gigging in the middle of the road for years and saw an opportunity in a new guise. The experienced and accomplished carried the disruptive stage stormers in what transpired to be an explosive blend.

Many of those who shot to prominence then on energy alone are now seasoned musicians, playing polished versions of classic three-chord rampages, often seated. It's damned difficult to be a musician for almost 50 years and not get better at it. Albeit refreshingly a few have managed.

Yet an emergent belief in the motivated, caffeinated amateur in large organizations negatively impacts many others within, as its performance deteriorates and brand evaporates. None is more depressing in this regard than the manager who feels as though with a bit more time they could do everyone's job better than the incumbent, and nothing more dispiriting than being on the receiving end of this exasperation. Especially when you know they couldn't and see quite clearly that they can barely even do their own. As referenced a number of times, with everything in corporate life, it's about balance. Spirit and energy entwined with the appropriate skills and knowledge. Start-ups know this, especially those that succeed. Yet in the corporate world that vital sliver of awareness is often casually dispensed with too. Which leaves those that remain to carry the burden and bear the consequences of under-achievement that inevitably result.

Un-f*cking self-image

Remaining immune from fads and trends takes more effort than falling in with them as we're pushing against the ubiquity of availability – of ideas and terms as much as tangible paraphernalia. When all the glamour appears to be channeled into the world of breakthrough megastars it feels like a televised talent show. They stand out for seeming to have their own mind, the courage and willingness to do things differently. We forget that in not wishing to put up with the crap they're creating their own crap. The start-up delusion is a challenge of self-image. Far from trying to be what we're not, we should re-state that:

~~"We're like a big start-up"~~

"We know where we're going, we never forget where we came from"

It's a recognition of where we're at. It looks both backward and forward, while acknowledging the present as the linkage. It simultaneously represents both a linear and non-linear view of time. Because tomorrow we'll be another day forward, yet the past and future will have altered and their influence on today re-calibrated. And if that's all just a tad conceptual, we can bank it and just avoid being an arse. No-one wants to work with an arse. We should remember that a significant advantage of being a start-up is being able to move fast without clawing through layers of risk-avoidance process. So with a will, we can stop being an arse with immediate effect.

Three potential ways to begin to un-fuck the misplaced, deranged and damaging failure of self-image manifested in the cult of start-up are as follows.

First, we're honest with ourselves. A start-up is generally less than 5 years old. After that it isn't a start-up. Not does it have anything of the start-up about it. It will be surviving on its merits, out of the funding rounds that got it there. It will be trying to do things decently and properly. It may still be a disruptor but will have a foot planted in the establishment it rattled. It will be in the public eye, so that some of the less desirable management practices will be patently evident. It's simply a young business. We acknowledge that by then it has its own personality, cultures and ways. All of which means we lay no claim to the territory at all.

Second, we tell better stories. Those that are from the organization and about the organization, not sourced from a social media inspired fantasy island. Stories of achievement, excellence and service through respect, consideration and decency. Demonstrating and reinforcing that it's entirely possible to be successful by being excellent to each other.

Third, we call out the crap. It will be there, in spades, it will seep through from external channels to everyday corporate parlance. Masks will be donned, acts perfected. We'll recognize the signs, the language, the behavior. We'll groan at the sight of adults at the school disco, those who should know better.

There's a chance that the entire fad for start-up will become so normalized it will be indistinguishable from expected organizational practice. Like the absorption of a subculture into the mainstream. Yet that may take some time. For now, if it's ignored it will proliferate, such is our tendency to mimic. If it's called out, we'll stand a chance. Even a small chance is worth taking.

Chapter 13

"This is a great place to work"

But it isn't. Is it?

We're almost done. Nothing covered so far has daunted us. We've navigated our way through it all, a little disheveled but unbowed. We've learned and grown, matured and relaxed into ourselves. We're excited by the present and optimistic about the future. Our colleagues are inspirational, and our leaders combine vision with commercial acumen, motivation with humanity. We're appreciated, recognized and rewarded and our ideas are heard and backed. Until the bloody screen in the meeting room won't connect to our laptop for a critical presentation that got moved six times because of ever-changing schedules. We came in on the hi-vis train and tried it at the crack of dawn and it worked. Now it doesn't. The helpdesk (not a desk, and no help) won't pick up. And because meetings are booked back-to-back, we're on. Now. It's a bloody nightmare. We're told not to sweat the small stuff, but it's the small stuff that kills us.

But yes, a "great place to work." A vacuous aspiration shared by so many, without embarrassment. One, even, that draws admiration. "Great" being an above-averageness that's entirely dependent upon an understanding and recognition of averageness. But many on that scale of averageness claim to be great. And not everyone can be. Other adjectives are notably avoided: fantastic, amazing, incredible, terrific or splendid may sound a little too far-fetched. And awesome is just garish and plasticky. It's a workplace, after all, not an amusement park. Even if the space does have a slide in reception, a climbing wall in the corner, a ball pit, table-tennis meeting tables and regular employees slither between open plan desks in that gibbon outfit.

Great is firm, sober and achievable. It leaves us with some space for work to get done when we're not unfolding for the day at a yoga class, re-centering in the mindfulness room, having the last frustrating meeting massaged out of our shoulders or making new best friends for life over a soya latte. Great is real.

All about the eXperience

As covered in Chapter 2, when we say "place" as a truncated version of "workplace" it's not just referring to the physical, it's the whole enchilada – people, space, culture and technology. How we relate to it has become termed the "workplace experience" (WX). It's more encompassing that the "employee experience," as it also includes all those with weaker ties to the organization. We're permitted a big X, other related terms such as UX (user experience) proudly display one.

They're all drawn from the idea of the "consumer experience," a broader trend of the sharing economy. In this we're driven more by the pursuit of "fantasies and fun," as the authors to first surface the idea, Morris Holbrook and Elizabeth Hirschman, identified in the subtitle of their paper in 1982[113], than the accumulation of stuff. It's about how we feel as consumers, the emotional impact, rather than the tangible reality. There's a narcissistic quality to it, too, as most of those moments tend to be captured on smartphones and shared on social media feeds for everyone to see and many to regret later, as what happens on the internet stays right there. "Look what a great experience I'm having, everyone!" It's quite likely that many lives are being viewed from both ends entirely through a 5-inch screen.

The idea of the dynamic, fluid and autobiographical positive workplace experience has therefore displaced the previously sacrosanct yet static and tinder-dry "employee value proposition" (EVP), usually formulated and formalized by HR. And so, organizations now instead desperately try to influence and curate this outcome, juggling liquid, to create a differentiated narrative. In a typical workplace there are, naturally, a highly limited number of components to play with. Despite the infinite comparisons, the workplace isn't a consumer offer. Employees aren't customers, no matter how hard we try and ram their collective foot into the glass slipper. And so, a once interesting idea, a more meaningful, rounded and accessible representation of organizational life than a one-dimensional scripted statement with a few germ-free stock photos, has become a geometrically expanding world of intolerable bullshit. Because "we're a great place to work."

It recalls the 1990 film *Crazy People* in which the main character, advertising executive Emory Leeson, suffers a nervous breakdown and creates a series of honest ads.[114] His colleagues check him into a psychiatric hospital, but his campaigns get published by mistake and are a huge success. Ads like "Volvo – they're boxy, but they're good." Eventually he turns the whole hospital into a branch of the ad agency, producing painfully honest straplines loved by the marketplace. Imagine a workplace experience being articulated in a similar manner.

This captures the entire problem with the "great place to work." Getting what matters right and being able to be honest about it is deemed not to be a differentiation because it's wrongly assumed that everyone else has it all completely sorted. Which they don't. Even though all the HR copywriters hang out at industry networking bashes and chew over the same problems. "Join us, we get the basics right" isn't much of a slogan for whatever the next generation may be termed to get excited about. It's the equivalent of "boxy but good." And so, claims are made for the most marginal attractions to entice those they mistakenly consider to be customers to their "brand." Whereas, if the pitch was that the role would be developmental to begin with and rewarded accordingly, then there would be opportunities in time for learning, career advancement and variety based on merit, that they would be valued and respected and treated fairly, and that while one or two colleagues may be hell-bent on pursuing their own twisted ends, the vast majority will enable and encourage the new appointee's progress, it could be a slam dunk. And if it's not, they probably weren't the right candidate for our organization.

So it should be with all the other aspects of a positive, functioning and effective workplace. Providing what's needed and making sure it's intuitive, easy to access and use, works for as much of the time as possible and when it doesn't is fixed as soon as it can be with advice on an alternative in the meantime. Starting with the things people need, and only when they're purring like Merlin the world-record breaking cat, considering what people want. That's quite a differentiation. It's rooted in the idea of the "minimum viable product" conceived in 2011 by Eric Ries, the stratospheric-selling originator of the lean start-up methodology.[115] It enables a proportionate amount of time to be devoted to functionality, reliability, usability and beauty (in that order of importance) to create a value-delivering product able to be tested by consumers without having to fully complete the whole thing before making it available. In simple terms, enough to be going on with.

It demands an effective feedback loop to enable co-creation – but with this, as a strategy, it works. On this basis we can envisage a "minimum viable workplace," getting everything needed right and only then considering what's wanted, building it purposefully – and together – as we go. As a client of the agency says in *Crazy People*: "Honesty. It's a terrific concept. We don't know much about it." It's time we knew more.

FFS-ers

We move to our day-to-day "experience" of our "great place to work." After we've given it the "benefit of the doubt." Like the audio visual issue we opened with, what lurks within is the cumulative erosion of our patience and energy through a series of events that, in isolation, may not appear to be anything but daily wear-and-tear. Minor inconveniences that we brush off without a thought, that may return in a lunchtime conversation about "that thing never working properly." Nothing that individually might trigger the need for advanced resilience training or a prolonged spell in the flotation tank. They're the natural rate of error or inefficiency in systems and processes that derive from the complexity of our working lives. The shit that happens.

They've been described as "micro-stressors" but they're far from "micro" when they eat a chunk out of a day that was already overloaded, cost us an opportunity we'd spent significant effort forging or ensured we missed our child's parent-teacher evening. This is the point in our reflection on work where we gather up the miscellaneous melancholy of the "place" (physical, digital and cultural) within which we labor that someone one day, in a polyester-clad moment of inspiration, decided to call "great." Of course, these stressors are all almost avoidable.

The lifecycle

It begins, of course, before we've begun. The "candidate experience." With some of this stuff we could honestly think we've had so long to get it right we should by now be getting it absolutely right. We're not innovating anything. We don't need highly specialized skill sets for the purpose. We just need to think it through from the candidate's point of view, end-to-end. As though we were the candidate. Which, of course, we were once, and might be again, but we seem to have forgotten. Or perhaps because we think everyone deserves to battle the obstacles we encountered.

As a first, vital step, the role has to have been approved in the first place, the obligatory signature chain complete. Then the role has to be positioned, predominantly online, to reflect what the job actually is and means. As much as is needed to avoid guesswork, paralyze with boredom or frighten senseless. Yet in many cases omitting the seniority and salary, the benchmarks by which most people gage their career path, to ensure as many people's time is wasted as possible and in case we can be bought cheaper, which is a throbbing red beacon. To the application process – setting it out in advance, responding promptly and respectfully, giving reasons where they're due, and providing contact email or heaven forbid an actual telephone number in case of questions, because for both parties *it's important*. Ensuring that the interviews are appropriate – numbers of attendees, structure, and the dignity of ensuring the interviewer has read our CV and supporting information in advance. And then with the final decision, actually making one in reasonable time (or at all) and being honest and open with those for whom it may go no further. If it's a success, warranting that the negotiation of terms is balanced and reasoned, and aligned with what was advertised.

If we're in, we're then subjected to the "onboarding experience." Again, this stuff isn't a surprise. "Oh, my heavens, we've got a new starter, what are we going to do with them? I'm really busy – can you handle it?" Of course, everyone's really busy, it's why you hired us. Imagine – we arrive on day one. We're met by someone who isn't dashing off to a meeting. We're given a company briefing, introduced to the key people we'll be working with, all of whom make time for us. Our kit is ready – security access, laptop, phone, business cards, applications, other relevant kit, all up and running – and we're shown where and how we'll be working, how the workplace works and how to do the key things like handle visitors, book rooms, operate equipment safely. We're taken for lunch, then shown the amenities and what we'll need to get the most out of them. And it's only 2pm. This is all normal, isn't it?

Beyond day one, we're into the "workplace experience" proper. We've started to find our way around. Even to do a bit of work. We're still in that can't-recall-anyone's-name phase but it's starting to form. Essentially what remains of the workplace experience after everything we've covered in this book is comprised of two interwoven areas – systems and processes, and the primary physical environment.

Before we get to those, to complete the lifecycle, it's the "departure experience." No-one much talks of it. We're not going to be told when we join what a great experience it is when we leave. It sounds a little related to the mortal coil. But when we're done, it's because of one of two reasons – we wanted to go, or the organization (more specifically, someone in it) wanted us to go. There can be a myriad of reasons for either path being pursued. The former – lack of opportunity, a better job elsewhere, a return to study, relocation, or something more worrying such as a personality clash, over-work or stress. Often the worrying stuff isn't declared in case it may prejudice a reference for a new role. The latter – performance issues, structural changes or cost-cutting. Either way there's likely to be emotion. The need for sensitivity is therefore vital at all stages. The "exit interview" is a critical opportunity for discovery, often hidden within its coded messaging. "It's been a great learning experience" means it was truly a regrettable hell. It's an area not to be neglected if it's to improve the experience of those whose life with the organization is about to begin.

Getting stuff done

Systems and processes break into two categories: the essential stuff, everything that we need to have in place, and the lovely stuff, which enriches our experience. We expect the former to work brilliantly because they're entirely unexciting. They rarely do, because the focus and investment is often on the latter category that comprises the marginal differentiation in the employee experience. The stuff that makes people want to join.

The essential stuff comprises the plethora of information and processes that remove the hassle from our day. From arrival, parking (if available), access and security, IT and phone kit and assistance, access to systems (like production, sales, purchasing), applications (such as holidays and absence), hardware, supplies, rooms and space, and the availability of resources and (if our role requires it) money. What we need is naturally where the problems often lie. There are four principal areas.

First, information. We need to know how to get stuff done. If it isn't forthcoming, we spend time and energy finding it. There appear to be two strategies at play. The first is *laissez-faire* need-to-know, enabled by word of mouth and who we know. The second is to provide all the necessary information in one easily accessible and intuitive place. But that involves investment. And so, the first method that has served the organization so well – stuff gets done doesn't it? – perpetuates. Any investment that's internal is always much harder to justify than that which is external, customer-facing and hence often revenue-driving. It's one stage removed, and we can't quantify the return. The frustration thus accumulates from the moment the onboarding experience is over. A negative workplace experience thereafter impacts the external customer experience. Who knew?

Second, simplicity and ease. If it takes a page of closely typed information to explain the operation of a light switch, it's dispiriting enough to ignore. We'll sit in the dark or go somewhere else. It needs to be immediately obvious and understandable. Our processes and methods must be logical, clear and make sense. Our personal investment in accessing and understanding them should be minimal. Rules and regulations should be only those needed to make it work, and no more. Designing something complex and then thinking it's been solved with information isn't sufficient or sustainable. Ensuring something is so complex that you're actually likely to lose the will to live before seeing it through – like raising a purchase order – isn't a smart deterrent either. It always leads to trouble.

While organizations are specifically designed to stop anyone spending any money, regardless of whether it's justified or necessary, complexity encourages the very workarounds it's introduced to prevent, placing those of us desperate to get our job done at undue risk.

Third, responsiveness. Nothing says "we care" more than a helpdesk ticket number. Or a notice saying the vital bit of kit we need right now is out of order. We can see it's out of order. When will it be back in order? In fact, even the very idea of a helpdesk brings us out in hives. A "one number" dial means at some point it must split into its channels – which means the numbered options of death. Press 9 to hear the interminable list all over again because your eyes glazed over halfway through. We want a real person, a living, breathing, vulnerable, imperfect and fragile soul before us, trained and competent, with whom we can converse, ask questions of, seek clarification. Maybe, even, get to know. And certainly, to thank.

Finally, fairness. In the "flat structure" that's often claimed, some people are less equal than others. And they get dispiritingly bumped. "Important" people get priority. Either because their competence in matters of everyday working life – like using a computer – is pitifully low and they need spoon-feeding, or because their time is more valuable. Or, rather, costing more. But it's entirely inverted. Those in daily direct customer contact are more likely to lose business than an executive behind a closed door watching the share price index twinkle. It's simpler and fairer for everyone to be treated as equally important and to receive equal service when required. Yet there will be a need, too, to elevate the needs of some people to ensure fairness. Working parents, for example. Their dependence on childcare or need to complete the school run may require arrangements to be made specifically to equalize provision, like parking spaces. Fairness demands proactivity.

The workplace

Above all else, a physical workplace has to be functional. It's a tool of the operation. It's not there for its own sake.

That first includes being able to get there, whether by public transport or vehicle, in the case of the latter necessitating the means to be able to park it safely (and affordably) nearby. Thereafter, form and function have been engaged in a running battle for the soul of the workplace for thousands of years, from which neither has emerged triumphant. The Roman architect Marcus Vitruvius Pollio in his book *De Architectura*, written in the first century BCE, stated that all things we create must possess stability (irmitatis), utility (utilitatis) and beauty (venustatis). They've become known as the "Vitruvian Virtues." There's a hint of the origin of the minimum viable product in the assertion, built on the foundation of functionality, working through stages toward beauty. The modern(ish) revival of the phrase is to be found in a beautiful statement by the American architect Louis Sullivan in 1896: "Whether it be the sweeping eagle in his flight, or the open apple-blossom, the toiling work-horse, the blithe swan, the branching oak, the winding stream at its base, the drifting clouds, over all the coursing sun, form ever follows function, and this is the law.[116]"

Clearly beauty can be a prime function, too, but only when the essential purpose of the workplace has been met. For those workplaces geared toward a specific purpose – hospitals, plants, factories, schools and the like – a non-functional outcome can be critical. That's not to say they won't be beset with problems, macro and micro. However, when we arrive at the office, with its highly generalized purpose, this is often where function and form curdle.

There are several key components of workplace functionality. It has to serve the intended core purpose of the activity to be undertaken in the space. In doing so it has to be simple, intuitive and easy to understand and navigate, and ensure the safety and health of all who will use it. And it has to work for everyone, however they are or choose to be, providing for diversity, inclusion and equality. There are no magic formulas or steps to follow in ensuring these tests are met. It's down to understanding and responding to the operational need (what it's for), an awareness of the challenges to be met (what it needs to do), excellent user-centered design (what it needs to comprise) and a focus on enabling service delivery when occupied (how to ensure it keeps working). It sounds so obvious, we're left to wonder how we often manage to get it so wrong.

Part of the overriding problem with the physical workplace is its inability to keep pace with the dynamism of the occupant organization and its environment. Creating physical space necessitates a lag from specification to completion, which may amount to years, and then an added lag from the moment the keys are handed over to a point at which it ceases to function as required and becomes counterproductive. As organizations become ever more dynamic, their workplace appears ever more rooted in an understanding of what was needed that has long since passed. While office dwellers have taken advantage of flexible space offers that can better support this dynamism, the same benefit isn't available in many other sectors. In such instances it places an increasing demand on service flexibility and response – and a necessity for all occupants to contribute, to be part of the dialog.

Un-f✱cking the experience

The entire experience of working for an organization ensures we interact over time with a number of people, each responsible for aspects that are required to seamlessly mesh for it to be beneficial, enjoyable and rewarding for everyone. We're probably one of those people, our actions benefiting others. As we established at the outset, "place" means the community of which we're part. The physical and digital environments are component parts. That means the employee experience is dependent upon everyone, whether they have a specific role in this regard or not. We all make it better for everyone else. The driver is the belonging. If we want to belong, we'll make sure everyone does. And we are our organization.

Our statement therefore re-emerges as:

"~~This is a great place to work~~"

"This is an organization we want to be part of"

It prompts as aspiration. And while it makes no specific claim to greatness, it implies that even where imperfections may be evident, work still very much in progress, we wish to be present, included and contributing. We feel connected and proud to be so. It's emotional. As it should be. Not just on the first and last day, but every day.

We can begin to un-fuck the workplace experience in three ways.

First, thinking, planning and acting as the consumer. We often forget we're in the mix too. We don't sit outside it, observing, we're not on Olympus messing with helpless mortal pawns. If something's crap for others it's likely crap for us. And vice versa. If not exactly now, we'll certainly remember. So why would we tolerate it? Just as the occupant organization exists in a state of "perpetual beta[117]" – an ever-evolving experiment in which all within are co-designers, evaluating and improving it – so too is the workplace in which it resides, whether we intend it that way or not. If we have any influence or control, everything should be created as if we're doing so for ourselves. Taking such an approach we'll often be surprised as to how incredibly particular we are. That's as good a guide and justification as any.

Second, we must never walk past anything. We'll see things

broken, half-broken, about to break, thinking of breaking if time permits. Or it could simply be much better than at present with little time, effort or expense applied, as we covered earlier. When we say "walk past," that applies to systems, processes, attitudes and behaviors – and not just walking, but interacting with or being aware of. We've identified the need to speak out at various junctures within this book – that's included here too. While our cumbersome modular organizational structures may appear to be a failsafe – everything is always someone's job, they'll find and get to it – it's often not. Or they don't pass this way or notice it. Or they see it and don't think it's broken. Or they simply don't care. In a workplace we're all responsible. It's what collegiality means. It's what being excellent to each other necessitates.

Third, we ensure everything works and we then build on what works. Never settling, never resting. The internal operating environment and the external environment in which an organization exists aren't unrelated ecosystems. In benefiting our experience within the organization, we directly benefit the external experience of customers or those with whom we interact or serve. That means competent, happy, committed, supported and motivated people, appropriately equipped and trained, evolving and innovating as the changing world in which they operate demands. We make sure everything we need is there, functioning, intuitive, easy to use. Then we begin to look at what we want to add or adapt. Or it simply all falls over. And no amount of third-rate copy is going to convince anyone otherwise. There's no earthly point in making a claim to be exceptional unless it can be substantiated; it will be seen through and exposed within moments. So we need to *be* exceptional. Because fundamentally, what works, works.

Which is great.

Chapter 14

We are where we're going

Work is still fucked. But we can now start to do something about it. Can't we?

Permit the author and collaborators a moment of reflection. Writing this book has been emotional. And in some small way, therapeutic. In thinking about its structure and content, we've worked through hundreds of situations in which we've found ourselves over the last 30 years and realized we still carry much of it with us. Which for all the emerging focus on wellbeing, isn't healthy. We rarely focus on the residual emotion, nestled in our gut, it only ever seems to be about *now*. We must expose it to expunge it. Perhaps therefore as you've been reading you've been doing the same and have seen something of a reflection of your own working life. However good work has been to you at times. Your own therapy.

What of that we've covered?

We can't say our analysis is different. Much of what we've evaluated has been critiqued before. But we've gathered it in one place to enable an understanding of each issue and its relationship with the others, to see how impenetrable and cloying the web can appear and to feel how lost we can be within it.

We can't say we've started something. The intent to un-fuck work has been going on as long as work itself. There are those actively campaigning for it, those whose practices set an example of a better way to which we can only aspire, and the lost millions who'd rather it was different, who feel unable to act. One way or the other, we're all involved. Wherever we are within the organization, whatever type of work we do and might want from it.

And we can't say it's definitive. The 12 statements cover most of the issues we face on a daily basis, but not all. There will be others. You'll have your own. We may need a second volume.

We've realized a few things along the way too.

The systems of work are stacked against us – the traditional, institutional, habitual. That doesn't make it impossible to change them. In our own sphere of activity, with the hope of generating a broader recognition that things can be different. But no-one's going to fix it for us. Protesting gets us nowhere. Expressed outrage is absorbed by the social machine, it invites, feeds and rewards it. Our objections, disgust, repugnance, are also all just content fodder. We have to *do* something.

It's difficult to face and admit that we're complicit, in our daily habits, in our ambivalence. Sometimes consciously, most often not, as we've accepted and habituated to the patterns we've found and created. But in being complicit, we can help ourselves. The key to the way in is the key to the way out. If we weren't, it would make it more difficult, it would be us against it all.

Which means that we're never "where we are" after all. We're never *being*, we're always *becoming*; adapting, evolving. Even when we feel mired, isolated, marooned. It's an idea as old as recorded philosophy but one that still requires advocacy. It's the essence of hope.

In a somewhat futile attempt at logical order, we've revealed 36 potential ways we might begin. Some of the re-cast phrases could point to more, but we've limited ourselves to three for each. But care is required. As we said at the outset, it's not a "36-point plan." It's not where this all began, a list at the kitchen table, the "things that must be done" as we'll all find things that need to be done. They've emerged from the process of demolition.

As everyone loves a "management summary," here it is:

Work

"~~Work is something we do, not a place we go~~"

"Work is something we do, something we create and a place we are"

We're always aware of our privilege and learn to see working life as others might.

We value "place" in its broadest sense as a physical, digital and collective experience, the energy of community.

We see all work as needed, and none devoid of meaning – and are restless in our commitment to ensuring it remains so.

Workload

"~~Hard work never hurt anyone~~"

"We're driven by purpose – and know our limits in pursuing it"

We value the quality of contribution and commitment over the quantity of time and effort.

Where we've required extra effort to be made, we always express gratitude.

We deem fairness the absolute barometer of workload, and as such the responsibility of us all.

Responsibility

"~~It's not a blame culture~~"

"We're all responsible – to ourselves and one another"

We become better humans so we can design better organizational systems.

We pursue understanding over blame, such that we can learn

from it.

Without question or consideration, where something is our fault, we raise our hand.

Trust
"~~We trust our people~~"

"We build trust"

We make trust a fundamental, inviolable condition of work, from the outset – it simply is.

We migrate from individual agendas to shared goal setting and evaluation – it's how we work.

We continually educate in what trust is and how to ensure it flourishes – we don't leave it to chance.

Equality
"~~We're an equal opportunities employer~~"

"We're striving to become an equitable organization"

We create awareness of inequality and its intersectionality – from here, we begin to roll it back.

From awareness we create a mass activism, an irresistible force for equality, appreciating and celebrating our differences.

We share stories – of what's working from which to learn, and what's not to understand and make it right.

Culture
"~~Culture eats strategy for breakfast~~"

"Culture makes strategy possible, strategy channels culture"

We're always excellent to one another – a disposition that

transcends culture.

We pursue diversity at every opportunity to create as broad a base as possible for our relations.

We recognize, understand and celebrate the many cultures within an organization, and resist the temptation to engineer the dominance of any one.

Innovation
"~~If it ain't broke, don't fix it~~"

"If it's broken we make it good, if it's good we make it better"

We see and recognize ideas for the unique and vital currency that they are and encourage them to surface.

We let Trojan mice run, to stimulate experimental creativity, respectfully challenging orthodoxies – and learn from what fails.

We maintain a restless curiosity and deploy critical thinking in respect of everything in our work.

Teams
"~~Teamwork makes the dream work~~"

"People, teams, organization: we know the time for each"

We establish where teams are necessary and ensure they're functional and a joy to be part of.

Where teams aren't necessary, we don't force fit them and the rituals associated.

We don't assume our team is the natural channel for an idea – it may need a new team, or no team at all.

Measurement
~~"If we can't measure it, we can't manage it"~~

"We measure and manage what we need – and guide the rest"

We define purpose of measurement, understanding each of why we need to measure, how we do so and what's needed.

We're careful with its use, understanding and defining the ground rules when we have it.

We're sparing with it, avoiding measuring what can't be or doesn't need to be, so we value what we do.

Management
~~"People are our greatest asset"~~

"We are our organization"

We build and sustain the value of management: why we need it, how it should be done and what it entails.

We treat people as human beings to be developed – not as assets to be maintained.

We cease referring to people as though we're not one of them, and acknowledge the organization is nothing without everyone within it.

Self-image
~~"We're like a big start-up"~~

"We know where we're going, we never forget where we came from"

We're honest with ourselves about who we are, where we are on our path and where we're heading.

We tell better stories from within the organization – of

excellence, decency and respect.

We call out the misguided and poor behavior that comes with the perpetuation of the myth of "start-up."

Workplace

"~~This is a great place to work~~"

"This is an organization we want to be part of"

To create and sustain a fantastic workplace we all think, plan and act as the consumer – we're involved.

We never walk past anything – broken, almost broken or deficient – we all look out for each other.

We ensure everything works and then build on what works – excellence is its own reward.

In a world of work where all these doors are open, we'll still have shitty days, do or say the wrong thing, upset someone we hadn't intended to, worry ourselves through the claustrophobia of the small hours, regret what we missed. But we'll be an activist among many for a better world of work: convinced, collegiate and committed. Fixing it for good.

Are you ready?

Petit fours

Perry's take

I wanted to believe it was good.

That, while recognizing it wasn't, it was because some people had corrupted it. Even temporarily. That it was snarly, dangerous, bites people, leaves a mess in its trail, is aggressive, loud and strikes fear into me, because it was wild not domesticated. I wanted to be the one to tame it. To show it love. To give it something it clearly needed: positive attention, hope, a sense of warmth and appreciation. I am only one and this wild beast is plural, a pack. A whole planet of dangerous predators.

I'm not talking about a timber wolf here. I'm talking about work.

I look at work like I do the wolf.

The order, the rituals, the pack-supporting mentality. The overcoming of adversity. The protection, the nurturing, the learning and the growing. The pack leader (alpha male) and the pack soul (the matriarch female). I also look at its beauty and sense of order in the world. And I look at its snarling teeth, its baying howl and its deeply frightening growl. I have respect for it and I appreciate it. I do, though, still want to pet it, to run with the pack, to lay down in safety and to playfully learn with the new generation.

But reading Neil's words caused two reactions in me aside from the creation of the wolf analogy. And he's kindly said it's a co-authored piece when in reality, because he's been more dedicated to it than I could be, it's 99 percent his work. Kirsten and I have been his initial audience. His reviewers. Not that he needs any, but also his validators.

Almost entirely of Neil's conceptualization, we concurred with his list of clichés, rituals or beliefs and marveled at his prose and his poetry. His extensive research, his linkages from concepts to reality; from abstract to hyper-connectedness. There's no way I could have positioned this content as elegantly or eloquently as he's done, yet I found myself in two states reading this book.

First, admiring the nature of the content and the exactness of his positions of this entire proposition – that work is fucked and has been for a long, long time. Now bear in mind my regard for the wolf as an analogy of actual work itself; this is hard for me to take. I am not in denial about work's present perilous state.

Quite the contrary. My very being in the work I do is actually to fix work. I would have no purpose if work were not in such a state of deplorable, desperate and damaged states. Because I want to do this doesn't give me any rights to sit above it all. And indeed I don't feel that nor ever will. I believe in what Neil has said with every ounce of my being, yet my working experience – two or three major incidents aside – has been joyous, fulfilling, defining. Yet I know I'm rare. If not weird.

It is partly what drives me to do the work I do now that I have the entity, my own enterprise, in doing this. I want to create similar experiences I have had for everyone else. I don't see myself as some fortunate isolated experiencer of a blessed life. I see that circumstances, my own choices, others around and a decent dollop of luck have gifted me the chances I've had in my work. I'm not alone, but there aren't many of us that can testify to this.

Second, feeling the tight knot in my stomach that I'm one of those privileged keyboard warrior knowledge workers that are the minority Neil refers to. And I'm in my bubble and naive belief that I am merely playing at being Luke Skywalker. That I won't save the universe with the proton torpedoes fired but guided by the force. I'll be more Wedge Antilles who pulled out because his engine was shot. Well intended, but peripheral.

Yet, as I said earlier, I exist to do something about it all.

So Neil and I conceived this book based on his convictions,

and I was merely the external manifestation of that someone you have the "napkin conversation" with for a new product. Or the part of the film team where a new movie concept was conceived. Neil is George Lucas, I'm more Frank Oz (the voice of Yoda). And yes, that makes Kirsten Carrie Fisher, perhaps.

So while I winced at some of this – so should you.

Because even from my stated mission, I've made work how it is. I've done shitty performance reviews. I've failed to acknowledge the craft of the ice cream vendor serving my marvelous sundae concoction.

Covid-19 made us all appreciate healthcare professionals, utility workers, delivery drivers, warehouse operatives and more. Yet even this hasn't un-fucked work. As we enter into hybrid office conversations we're ignoring those in agriculture, energy provision and logistics haulers who've kept us all going in a year of static safety.

This isn't a virtue-signaling book so we clap on a Thursday. This is a serious call for everyone who has anything to do with work to stop with the screwed up version we have and do something about it.

Neil's so cleverly alluded to how, but left it to you.

Because it's taken thousands of years of constant aggregated fuckery to get it here. So we aren't going to turn the ship around in a blink. Instead though, we ALL have to do something hourly, daily, weekly, monthly, yearly even.

Fixing work isn't to topple oligarchic demi-gods of industry, but to channel ourselves toward that sense of something I believe was defined for us as long ago as fifth-century BCE Greece: eudaimonia – human flourishing. Fulfilled, healthy, balanced lives. In doing so we make ready for the next intake, who can inherit and accelerate an emergence.

What are you doing to make it happen?

Kirsten's take

Eleven years deep into the "world of work." A young un' according to some, yet also tagged as being within "the next gen of leaders." What I did not know when I entered the workplace in 2010, having graduated and seeking the coveted "grad schemes" of a recession ridden world, I wish I did. Naivety can be a blessing, but where our twenty-first century workplaces are concerned, there are long established practices, habits, behaviors and politics one has one's eyes opened to.

When asked to be a part of Neil and Perry's book project, I was beyond thrilled. I reviewed this, avidly, and with each chapter recognized aspects which had been exemplified in my own experience of the workplace.

These issues exist. Everywhere. Whether in the smallest of incidences, or in droves. They exist. The ills of society manifest themselves in the workplace for the workplace is a microcosm of society. The workplace as we know it is therefore a microcosm of a Victorian-era work system, adapted, or should I say contorted, to fit our twenty-first century lifestyle. The system is – excuse my language Mum and Dad – fucked. And as with all systems, they degrade, and if they don't evolve in accordance with human requirements, they break.

And I believe that many workplaces are, sadly, broken. I have heard about it, seen it, felt it. These broken systems steam ahead, however; weakening overall performance, employee engagement, and worst of all, human spirit. Neil's book articulates so beautifully and profoundly why we must recognize these weakened, if not broken, aspects of the work we know, and how, with a shift in mindset we can repair, or – lo and behold – reinvent them.

As the Millennial among this wolf tribe, I have the longest serving tenure ahead. I want to see the next 40-plus years of my career as an anticipated challenge, not a life sentence to the cause of work. The reality for many of us is that we will spend hours upon hours working for others in charge, enabling wealth; profiting from our skills, commitment and unintended fueling of the system we see. I believe that if we – as Perry alluded to in his take – can pair our personal passions with people who put purpose ahead of profit, the world of work can see a seismic shift where we future-proof our world, and not just our businesses.

In my role as Chief Impact Officer at PTHR, that is what we aim to do. In our micro-consultancy we seek to be sustainable; economically, socially and environmentally. We're able to act this way through adhering to our principles, for example, having guidance on companies and charities we will work with and support; through having a publicly professed "Pledge to Our Planet"; and through meaningful connections with our talented and loving network, Neil a prominent member of this.

I am so grateful to Neil and Perry for my inclusion in the creation of this piece of poetic provocation. I urge all Millennials to read this, not to cause fear or rebuttal of their workplace, but to heighten awareness that problems exist and that they can be changed. One conversation can stir the soul.

And from there – says the optimist – anything is possible.

Endnotes

Chapter 1

1   Kurt Vonnegut, *Breakfast of Champions* (London: Random House, 2009).

2   Athena is a UK retail outlet founded in 1964 – now online only – selling fine art. It became famous in the 1970s and 1980s for its affordable prints of iconic photographic images.

Chapter 2

3   Jack Nilles, *The Telecommunications-Transportation Tradeoff* (Createspace Independent Publishing, 2007).

4   David Streitfeld, "The long, unhappy history of working from home," *New York Times*, 29 June 2020, https://www.nytimes.com/2020/06/29/technology/working-from-home-failure.html (accessed 20 March 2021).

5   Richard Daft and Robert Lengel, "Organizational information requirements, media richness and structural design," *Management Science* 32 (5), 1986.

6   Peter Drucker, *The Landmarks of Tomorrow* (London: Harper, 1959).

7   "Employment and employment types," Office for National Statistics, n.d., https://www.ons.gov.uk/employmentandlabourmarket/peopleinwork/employmentandemployeetypes (accessed 20 March 2021).

8   "Ethnicity facts and figures," *UK Government*, 15 May 2000, https://www.ethnicity-facts-figures.service.gov.uk/work-pay-and-benefits/employment/employment-by-occupation/latest (accessed 20 March 2021).

9   Emma Keller, "Yahoo CEO Marissa Mayer's work-from-home memo is from bygone era," *The Guardian*, 26 February 2013, https://www.theguardian.com/commentisfree/2013/feb/26/yahoo-ceo-marissa-mayer-memo-telecommute (accessed 20 March 2021).

10 Julianne Pepitone, "Best Buy ends its work-from-home program,"

CNN Money, March 2103, https://money.cnn.com/2013/03/05/technology/best-buy-work-from-home/ (accessed 20 March 2021).

11 John Simons, "IBM, a Pioneer of Remote Work, Calls Workers Back to the Office" *Wall Street Journal*, 18 March 2017, https://www.wsj.com/articles/ibm-a-pioneer-of-remote-work-calls-workers-back-to-the-office-1495108802?mg=id-wsj (accessed 20 March 2021).

12 Charles Handy, "My Ideal Office," *Idler*, 7 August 2020, https://www.idler.co.uk/article/charles-handy-club-culture/ (accessed 20 March 2021).

13 Peter Currell Brown, *Smallcreep's Day* (London: Pinter & Martin, 2008).

14 Franz Kafka, *The Castle* (Harmondsworth: Penguin Classics, 2015).

15 "Marx's Theory of Alienation," *Wikipedia*, n.d., https://en.wikipedia.org/wiki/Marx%27s_theory_of_alienation (accessed 6 March 2021).

16 Julia Hobsbawm, *The Nowhere Office* (London: Demos, March 2021).

17 "Women shoulder the responsibility of unpaid work," *Office for National Statistics*, 10 November 2016, https://www.ons.gov.uk/employmentandlabourmarket/peopleinwork/earningsandworkinghours/articles/womenshouldertheresponsibilityofunpaidwork/2016-11-10 (accessed 20 March 2021).

18 Claire Cain Miller, "How society pays when women's work is unpaid," *New York Times*, 22 February 2016, https://www.nytimes.com/2016/02/23/upshot/how-society-pays-when-womens-work-is-unpaid.html (accessed 20 March 2021).

19 Max Stirner, *The Ego and its Own* (New York: Verso Books, 2014).

20 Adam Uzialko, "How to manage workplace relationships," *Business News Daily*, 2 March 2019, https://www.businessnewsdaily.com/7764-co-workers-dating.html (accessed 20 March 2021).

21 Eva M. Krockow, "How many decisions do we make each day?" *Psychology Today*, 27 September 2018, https://www.psychologytoday.com/us/blog/stretching-theory/201809/how-many-decisions-do-we-make-each-day (accessed 20 March 2021).

.

Chapter 3

22 Emile Zola, *L'Assommoir*, trans. Leonard Tancock (Harmondsworth: Penguin, 1970).

23 "Eight-Hour Day," *Wikipedia*, https://en.wikipedia.org/wiki/Eight-hour_day (accessed 20 March 2021).

24 Frank Pega et al, "Global, regional, and national burdens of ischemic heart disease and stroke attributable to exposure to long working hours for 194 countries, 2000–2016," *Environment International*, 17 May 2021, https://www.sciencedirect.com/science/article/pii/S0160412021002208 (accessed 5 June 2021).

25 Graham Greene, *A Burnt Out Case* (London: Vintage Classics, 2004).

26 Perry Timms, *The Energized Workplace* (London: Kogan Page, 2020).

27 Addley, Esther, and Laura Barton. "Who Said Hard Work Never Hurt Anybody?" *Guardian News and Media*, 13 March 2001, https://www.theguardian.com/money/2001/mar/13/workandcareers.japan (accessed 20 March 2021).

28 Sally Adee, "Mustn't grumble," *The Last Word On Nothing*, https://www.lastwordonnothing.com/2014/01/24/mustnt-grumble/ (accessed 5 June 2021).

29 Ben Zimmer, "The Meaning of 'Man Up.'" *The New York Times*, 3 September 2010, 2021. https://www.nytimes.com/2010/09/05/magazine/05FOB-onlanguage-t.html (accessed 20 March 2021).

30 C Northcote Parkinson, *Parkinson's Law* (Cambridge: Houghton Mifflin Co., 1957).

31 "History of Stress," *CESH/CSHS*, 17 August 2017. https://humanstress.ca/stress/what-is-stress/history-of-stress/ (accessed 20 March 2021).

Chapter 4

32   "Road Traffic Injuries," *World Health Organisation*, 7 February 2020, https://www.who.int/news-room/fact-sheets/detail/road-traffic-injuries (accessed 20 March 2021).

33   "High Reliability Organization," *Wikipedia*, n.d., https://en.wikipedia.org/wiki/High_reliability_organization (accessed 20 March 2021).

34   "What does a no blame culture actually look like?" *Investors in People*, n.d., https://www.investorsinpeople.com/knowledge/no-blame-culture-actually-look-like/ (accessed 20 March 2021).

35   Colin Ward, *Anarchy in Action* (London: Allen & Unwin, 1973).

36   "Holacracy Constitution," *Holacracy*, n.d. https://www.holacracy.org/constitution (accessed 20 March 2021).

37   "Holons," *Wikipedia*, n.d., https://en.wikipedia.org/wiki/Holon_(philosophy) (accessed 27 February 2021).

38   Arthur Koestler, *The Ghost in the Machine* (London: Pan Books, 1970).

39   Daniel Pink, *Drive* (New York: Riverhead Books, 2009).

40   Pim de Morree, "Bursting the Bubble: Teal Ain't Real," *Corporate Rebels*, 2018, https://corporate-rebels.com/teal-aint-real/ (accessed 20 March 2021).

41   "The Most Exciting Phrase in Science Is Not 'Eureka!' But 'That's funny ...,'" *Quote Investigator*, n.d., https://quoteinvestigator.com/2015/03/02/eureka-funny/ (accessed 20 March 2021).

42   Katherine Ellen Foley, "Viagra's famous surprising origin," *Quartz*, 10 September 2017, https://qz.com/1070732/viagras-famously-surprising-origin-story-is-actually-a-pretty-common-way-to-find-new-drugs/ (accessed 20 March 2021).

Chapter 5

43   Niccolò Machiavelli, *The Prince* (Oxford: Oxford University Press, 1984).

44   Geoffrey Hosking "Why we need a history of trust," *Reviews in History*, July 2002, https://reviews.history.ac.uk/review/287a

(accessed 20 March 2021).

45   Thomas Hobbes, *Leviathan* (Ware: Wordsworth Editions, 2014).

46   Ernest Hemingway, Ernest Hemingway Selected Letters: 1917–
      1961, ed. Carlos Baker (New York: Ernest Hemingway Foundation,
      Inc., 1981).

47   William A. Kahn, "Psychological Conditions of Personal
      Engagement and Disengagement at Work," Academy of
      Management Journal 33, no. 4 (1990): 692–724.

48   Alex Rosenblat, Tamara Kneese, and Danah Boyd, "Workplace
      Surveillance" Data & Society Working Paper, 8 October 2014
      https://www.datasociety.net/pubs/fow/WorkplaceSurveillance.
      pdf (accessed 20 March 2021).

49   Mark Eltringham, "At least nobody is whinging about open
      plan offices anymore," *Workplace Insight*, 6 March 2021, https://
      workplaceinsight.net/well-at-least-nobody-is-whinging-about-
      open-plan-offices-anymore/ (accessed 20 March 2021).

Chapter 6

50   Jason Willick, "The man who discovered culture wars," *Wall Street
      Journal*, 25 May 2018 https://www.wsj.com/articles/the-man-who-
      discovered-culture-wars-1527286035 (accessed 20 March 2021).

51   Linda Scott, *The Double X Economy* (London: Faber & Faber, 2020).

52   Caroline Criado Perez, *Invisible Women* (London: Chatto & Windus,
      2019).

53   Mary Beard, *Women & Power: A Manifesto* (London: Profile Books,
      2017).

54   V (formerly Eve Ensler), "Disaster patriarchy: how the pandemic
      has unleashed a war on women," *The Guardian*, 1 June 2021,
      https://www.theguardian.com/lifeandstyle/2021/jun/01/disaster-
      patriarchy-how-the-pandemic-has-unleashed-a-war-on-women
      (accessed 1 June 2021).

55   Bailey Reiners, "12 Unconscious bias examples and how to avoid
      them in the workplace," *Built In*, 1 February 2021, https://builtin.
      com/diversity-inclusion/unconscious-bias-examples (accessed 20

March 2021).

56   Maya Oppenheim, "Coronavirus crisis drives gender inequality," *The Independent*, 15 July 2020, https://www.independent.co.uk/ independentpremium/uk-news/coronavirus-job-losses-women-gender-inequality-exeter-study-a9620461.html (accessed 20 March 2021).

57   Jill Lepore, "What's wrong with the way we work," *New Yorker*, 11 January 2021, https://www.newyorker.com/magazine/2021/01/18/ whats-wrong-with-the-way-we-work (accessed 20 March 2021).

58   Kate Usher, *Your Second Phase* (London: LID Publishing, 2020).

59   Hilary Osborne, "A third of women hide menopause symptoms at work – report" *The Guardian*, 9 March 2021, https://www. theguardian.com/society/2021/mar/08/a-third-of-women-hide-menopause-symptoms-at-work-report (accessed 20 March 2021).

60   Paul Hill, "Busting the Margaret Thatcher Voice Coaching Myth," *Working Voices*, 12 April 2013, https://www.workingvoices.com/ insights/busting-the-margaret-thatcher-voice-coaching-myth/ (accessed 20 March 2021).

61   Arthur Schopenhauer, *Essays and Aphorisms*, trans. R. J. Hollingdale (Harmondsworth: Penguin Books, 1970).

62   Margaret Atwood, *The Handmaid's Tale* (New York: 1985).

63   Jenny Little, "Ten years on why are there still so few women in tech?" *The Guardian*, 2 January 2020, https://www.theguardian. com/careers/2020/jan/02/ten-years-on-why-are-there-still-so-few-women-in-tech (accessed 20 March 2021).

64   Jenny Little (2021).

65   Sarah White, "Women in tech statistics," *CIO*, 23 January 2020, https://www.cio.com/article/3516012/women-in-tech-statistics-the-hard-truths-of-an-uphill-battle.html (accessed 20 March 2021).

66   Laura Hood, "Research shows that four in five experts cited in online news are men," *The Conversation*, 19 July 2018, https:// theconversation.com/research-shows-four-in-five-experts-cited-in-online-news-are-men-100207 (accessed 20 March 2021).

67   Anne M Koenig "Comparing Prescriptive and Descriptive

Gender Stereotypes About Children, Adults, and the Elderly," *Frontiers in Psychology*, 26 June 2018, https://www.frontiersin.org/articles/10.3389/fpsyg.2018.01086/full (accessed 20 March 2021).

68   Jack Zenger and Joseph Folkman, "Research: Women are better leaders during a crisis," *Harvard Business Review*, 30 December 2020 https://hbr.org/2020/12/research-women-are-better-leaders-during-a-crisis (accessed 20 March 2021).

69   "Gender pay gap in the UK" *Office for National Statistics*, n.d., https://www.ons.gov.uk/employmentandlabourmarket/peopleinwork/earningsandworkinghours/bulletins/genderpaygapintheuk/2020 (accessed 20 March 2021).

70   "What is the gender pension gap?" *Prospect*, 3 March 2021, https://prospect.org.uk/article/what-is-the-gender-pension-gap/ (accessed 20 March 2021).

71   "10 facts about women and caring in the UK on International Women's Day," *Carers UK*, 7 March 2021, https://www.carersuk.org/news-and-campaigns/campaigns/carers-rights-day/29-news-campaigns/stories/5156-10-facts-about-women-and-caring-in-the-uk-on-international-women-s-day (accessed 20 March 2021).

Chapter 7

72   "Culture eats strategy for breakfast," *Quote Investigator* https://quoteinvestigator.com/2017/05/23/culture-eats/ (accessed 20 March 2021).

73   "Garden of the Arcane Delights" was the first EP released by Australian band Dead Can Dance on 4AD records in August 1984. It's very good.

74   Martin Bower, "Company philosophy: 'The way we do things around here,'" *McKinsey*, 1 May 2003, https://www.mckinsey.com/featured-insights/leadership/company-philosophy-the-way-we-do-things-around-here (accessed 20 March 2021).

75   Don Mitchell, "There's No Such Thing as Culture: Towards a Reconceptualization of the Idea of Culture in Geography," *Transactions of the Institute of British Geographers*, New Series, Vol.

20, No. 1. 1995, pp. 102-116.

76 "The Cultural Web," *Mind Tools*, n.d., https://www.mindtools. com/pages/article/newSTR_90.htm (accessed 20 March 2021).

77 Zygmunt Bauman, *Culture as Praxis* (London: Sage, 1999).

78 Thomas Carlyle, *On Heroes, Hero-Worship, and The Heroic in History* (Scotts Valley: CreateSpace Independent Publishing, 2018).

79 James Gill, "The death of Sub-culture, part 7," *Further*, 19 December 2017, https://www.further.co.uk/blog/death-of-subculture-part-7-subculture-becoming-culture-neotribalism-whats-the-next-subculture/ (accessed 20 March 2021).

80 Karl Marx, "A Contribution to the Critique of Hegel's Philosophy of Right" *Marxists*, n.d., https://www.marxists.org/archive/marx/works/1843/critique-hpr/intro.htm (accessed 20 March 2021).

81 Paul Lopushinsky, "Forced fun in the workplace is no fun," *Playficient*, 18 July 2020, https://www.playficient.com/forced-fun/ (accessed 20 March 2021).

82 Barbara Plester and Helena Cooper-Thomas, "The fun paradox," *Employee Relations, Volume 37*, 27 April 2015.

Chapter 8

83 J. Murdock, "Humans have more than 6,000 thoughts per day, psychologists discover," *Newsweek*. 15 July 2020, https://www.newsweek.com/humans-6000-thoughts-every-day-1517963 (accessed 20 March 2021).

84 "The meaning and origin of the phrase: if it ain't broke don't fix it." *The Phrase Finder*, n.d., https://www.phrases.org.uk/meanings/if-it-aint-broke-dont-fix-it.html (accessed 20 March 2021).

85 Gregory Y Titelman, *Random House Dictionary of Popular Proverbs and Sayings* (New York: Random House, 1966).

86 Lucy Jones, "Are there some animals that have stopped evolving?" *BBC*, 13 April 2015, http://www.bbc.co.uk/earth/story/20150413-can-an-animal-stop-evolving (accessed 20 March 2021).

87 J. Kellstadt, "The Necessity and Impossibility of Anti-Activism," *The Anarchist Library*, 2021, https://theanarchistlibrary.org/library/

j-kellstadt-the-necessity-and-impossibility-of-anti-activism (accessed 20 March 2021).

88   Euan Semple, *Organisations Don't Tweet, People Do: A Manager's Guide to the Social Web* (London: Wiley & Sons, 2012).

Chapter 9

89   Sociometry is a quantitative method for measuring social relationships created by Jacob Moreno and Helen Hall Jennings in the 1950s.

90   John C. Maxwell, *Teamwork Makes the Dream Work* (Petaling Jaya: Advantage Quest Publications, 2008).

91   K. L. Unsworth and M. A. West. "Teams: The challenges of cooperative work," in N. Chmiel (Ed.), *An introduction to work and organizational psychology: A European perspective"* (Oxford: Blackwell Publishing, 2000).

92   Jack Groppel, *The Corporate Athlete: How to Achieve Maximal Performance in Business and Life* (London: Wiley & Sons, 1999).

93   Jim Loehr and Tony Schwartz, "The making of a corporate athlete," *Harvard Business Review*, January 2001, https://hbr.org/2001/01/the-making-of-a-corporate-athlete (accessed 20 March 2021).

94   "Designing Effective Collaboration," *Economist Intelligence Unit*, 2008, http://graphics.eiu.com/marketing/pdf/Cisco%20Collaboration.pdf (accessed 20 March 2021).

95   Charles Duhigg, "What Google learned from its quest to build the perfect team," *New York Times*, 25 February 2106, https://www.nytimes.com/2016/02/28/magazine/what-google-learned-from-its-quest-to-build-the-perfect-team.html (accessed 20 March 2021).

96   Paul Graham, "Manager's schedule, maker's schedule," *Paul Graham*, July 2009, http://www.paulgraham.com/makersschedule.html (accessed 20 March 2021).

Chapter 10

97   Stafford Beer, *The Brain of the Firm* (London: Wiley & Sons, 1981).

98   Frederick Winslow Taylor (1856–1915) was an engineer who was

among the first to work toward efficiency in the workplace, and the originator of time-and-motion studies – see https://www.britannica.com/biography/Frederick-W-Taylor (accessed 20 March 2021).

99 Rachael Reeves, "Donald Trump's presidential counsellor Kellyanne Conway says Sean Spicer gave 'alternative facts' at first press briefing," *The Independent*, 22 January 2018, https://www.independent.co.uk/news/world/americas/kellyanne-conway-sean-spicer-alternative-facts-lies-press-briefing-donald-trump-administration-a7540441.html (accessed 20 March 2021).

100 Peter Currell Brown (2008).

101 Lakshmi, Rama "Applying Meaning to Management With Ancient Hindu Mythology," *Washington Post*, 26 January 2009, http://www.washingtonpost.com/wp-dyn/content/article/2009/01/25/AR20090125021 (accessed 20 March 2021).

102 Liz Ryan, "'If You Can't Measure It, You Can't Manage It': Not True." *Forbes Magazine*, 10 February 2014, https://www.forbes.com/sites/lizryan/2014/02/10/if-you-cant-measure-it-you-cant-manage-it-is-bs/?sh=518db4f77b8b (accessed 20 March 2021).

Chapter 11

103 Li Jin, "Unbundling work from employment," *Li's Newsletter*, 20 June 2020, https://li.substack.com/p/unbundling-work-from-employment (accessed 20 March 2021).

104 William Whyte, *The Organization Man* (Pennsylvania: University of Pennsylvania Press, 2002).

105 Laurence J. Peter, *The Peter Principle: How things go wrong* (Michigan: W Morrow, 1969).

106 David Owen, "Customer satisfaction at the push of a button," *New Yorker*, 20 January 2018, https://www.newyorker.com/magazine/2018/02/05/customer-satisfaction-at-the-push-of-a-button (accessed 20 March 2021).

Chapter 12

107 "Startup History," *Starting Up*, n.d., https://starting-up.org/en/

starting-up/introduction/startup-history/ (accessed 20 March 2021).

108 Sean Bryant, "How Many Start-ups Fail and Why?" *Investopedia*, 9 November 2020, https://www.investopedia.com/articles/personal-finance/040915/how-many-startups-fail-and-why.asp (accessed 20 March 2021).

109 Luke Haines, *Bad Vibes: Britpop and my part in its downfall* (London: Windmill Books, 2010).

110 Timothy Bella, "'Just Do It': The Surprising and Morbid Origin Story of Nike's Slogan," *The Washington Post*, 29 March 2019, https://www.washingtonpost.com/news/morning-mix/wp/2018/09/04/from-lets-do-it-to-just-do-it-how-nike-adapted-gary-gilmores-last-words-before-execution/ (accessed 20 March 2021).

111 Natalie Robehmed, "What Is A Startup?" *Forbes Magazine*, 15 May 2015, https://www.forbes.com/sites/natalierobehmed/2013/12/16/what-is-a-startup/ (accessed 20 March 2021).

112 Annebella Pollen, "Why the KLF burned one million pounds in 1994," *52 Insights*, 1 September 2017, https://www.52-insights.com/news/why-the-klf-burnt-1-million-pounds-in-1994/ (accessed 20 March 2021).

Chapter 13

113 Morris Holbrook and Elizabeth Hirschman, "The experiential aspects of consumption: Consumer fantasies, feelings and fun," *Journal of Consumer Research*, 9:2, 1982.

114 "Crazy People," *IMDB*, n.d., https://www.imdb.com/title/tt0099316/ (accessed 20 March 2021).

115 Eric Ries, *The Lean Startup* (London: Portfolio Penguin, 2011).

116 Louis Sullivan, "The Tall Office Building Artistically Considered," *Lippincott's Monthly Magazine*, No 57(1896) p. 403-409.

117 Tim O'Reilly and John Battelle, "What is Web 2.0?" *O'Reilly*, https://www.oreilly.com/pub/a/web2/archive/what-is-web-20.html?page=4 30 September 2005 (accessed 20 March 2021).

Biographies

Kirsten, Perry and Neil have had some jobs, done some good stuff, messed some stuff up, been promoted, been remonstrated with, made some decisions they probably shouldn't have or weren't allowed to, had some ideas, pushed some boundaries, made some money, spent some money, been good managers, been crap managers, ignored some signs, learned some lessons, listened, not listened, been pushed under the bus, driven the bus, got annoyed about things they shouldn't have and not got annoyed about things they should have. All in a typical week.

If you want to know more about us, you'll find us on LinkedIn.

Thank you for buying this book. Or for picking it up when you found it on a train. If you like what you've read, we'd be delighted if you'd pop a review on your website of choice. If you didn't, please feel free to tell us why:

neilusher@hotmail.com
@workessence

kirsten@pthr.co.uk
@KirstenKiwi

perry@pthr.co.uk
@PerryTimms

In fact, please drop us a line anyway and let us know what you thought. It would be massively appreciated, and would be great to connect.

Keep a look out for volume 2.

CULTURE, SOCIETY & POLITICS

Contemporary culture has eliminated the concept and public figure of the intellectual. A cretinous anti-intellectualism presides, cheer-led by hacks in the pay of multinational corporations who reassure their bored readers that there is no need to rouse themselves from their stupor. Zer0 Books knows that another kind of discourse - intellectual without being academic, popular without being populist - is not only possible: it is already flourishing. Zer0 is convinced that in the unthinking, blandly consensual culture in which we live, critical and engaged theoretical reflection is more important than ever before.

If you have enjoyed this book, why not tell other readers by posting a review on your preferred book site.

You may also wish to
subscribe to our Zer0 Books YouTube Channel.

Bestsellers from Zer0 Books include:

Give Them An Argument
Logic for the Left
Ben Burgis
Many serious leftists have learned to distrust talk of logic. This
is a serious mistake.
Paperback: 978-1-78904-210-8 ebook: 978-1-78904-211-5

Poor but Sexy
Culture Clashes in Europe East and West
Agata Pyzik
How the East stayed East and the West stayed West.
Paperback: 978-1-78099-394-2 ebook: 978-1-78099-395-9

An Anthropology of Nothing in Particular
Martin Demant Frederiksen
A journey into the social lives of meaninglessness.
Paperback: 978-1-78535-699-5 ebook: 978-1-78535-700-8

In the Dust of This Planet
Horror of Philosophy vol. 1 Eugene Thacker
In the first of a series of three books on the Horror of
Philosophy, *In the Dust of This Planet* offers the genre of horror
as a way of thinking about the unthinkable.
Paperback: 978-1-84694-676-9 ebook: 978-1-78099-010-1

The End of Oulipo?
An Attempt to Exhaust a Movement
Lauren Elkin, Veronica Esposito
Paperback: 978-1-78099-655-4 ebook: 978-1-78099-656-1

Capitalist Realism
Is There No Alternative?
Mark Fisher
An analysis of the ways in which capitalism has presented
itself as the only realistic political-economic system.
Paperback: 978-1-84694-317-1 ebook: 978-1-78099-734-6

Rebel Rebel
Chris O'Leary
David Bowie: every single song. Everything you want to know,
everything you didn't know.
Paperback: 978-1-78099-244-0 ebook: 978-1-78099-713-1

Kill All Normies
Angela Nagle
Online culture wars from 4chan and Tumblr to Trump.
Paperback: 978-1-78535-543-1 ebook: 978-1-78535-544-8

Cartographies of the Absolute
Alberto Toscano, Jeff Kinkle
An aesthetics of the economy for the twenty-first century.
Paperback: 978-1-78099-275-4 ebook: 978-1-78279-973-3

Malign Velocities
Accelerationism and Capitalism
Benjamin Noys
Long listed for the Bread and Roses Prize 2015, *Malign
Velocities* argues against the need for speed, tracking
acceleration as the symptom of the ongoing crises of
capitalism.
Paperback: 978-1-78279-300-7 ebook: 978-1-78279-299-4

Meat Market
Female Flesh under Capitalism
Laurie Penny
A feminist dissection of women's bodies as the fleshy fulcrum
of capitalist cannibalism, whereby women are both consumers
and consumed.
Paperback: 978-1-84694-521-2 ebook: 978-1-84694-782-7

Babbling Corpse
Vaporwave and the Commodification of Ghosts
Grafton Tanner
Paperback: 978-1-78279-759-3 ebook: 978-1-78279-760-9

New Work New Culture
Work we want and a culture that strengthens us
Frithjof Bergmann
A serious alternative for mankind and the planet.
Paperback: 978-1-78904-064-7 ebook: 978-1-78904-065-4

Romeo and Juliet in Palestine
Teaching Under Occupation
Tom Sperlinger
Life in the West Bank, the nature of pedagogy and the role of a
university under occupation.
Paperback: 978-1-78279-637-4 ebook: 978-1-78279-636-7

Color, Facture, Art and Design
Iona Singh
This materialist definition of fine-art develops guidelines for
architecture, design, cultural-studies and ultimately social
change.
Paperback: 978-1-78099-629-5 ebook: 978-1-78099-630-1

Sweetening the Pill
or How We Got Hooked on Hormonal Birth Control Holly
Grigg-Spall
Has contraception liberated or oppressed women?
Sweetening the Pill breaks the silence on the dark side of
hormonal contraception.
Paperback: 978-1-78099-607-3 ebook: 978-1-78099-608-0

Why Are We The Good Guys?
Reclaiming Your Mind from the Delusions of Propaganda
David Cromwell
A provocative challenge to the standard ideology that Western
power is a benevolent force in the world.
Paperback: 978-1-78099-365-2 ebook: 978-1-78099-366-9

The Writing on the Wall
On the Decomposition of Capitalism and its Critics Anselm
Jappe, Alastair Hemmens
A new approach to the meaning of social emancipation.
Paperback: 978-1-78535-581-3 ebook: 978-1-78535-582-0

Enjoying It
Candy Crush and Capitalism
Alfie Bown
A study of enjoyment and of the enjoyment of studying. Bown
asks what enjoyment says about us and what we say about
enjoyment, and why.
Paperback: 978-1-78535-155-6 ebook: 978-1-78535-156-3

Ghosts of My Life
Writings on Depression, Hauntology and Lost Futures
Mark Fisher
Paperback: 978-1-78099-226-6 ebook: 978-1-78279-624-4

Neglected or Misunderstood
The Radical Feminism of Shulamith Firestone
Victoria Margree
An interrogation of issues surrounding gender, biology,
sexuality, work and technology, and the ways in which our
imaginations continue to be in thrall to ideologies of maternity
and the nuclear family.
Paperback: 978-1-78535-539-4 ebook: 978-1-78535-540-0

How to Dismantle the NHS in 10 Easy Steps (Second Edition)
Youssef El-Gingihy
The story of how your NHS was sold off and why you will
have to buy private health insurance soon. A new expanded
second edition with chapters on junior doctors' strikes and
government blueprints for US-style healthcare.
Paperback: 978-1-78904-178-1 ebook: 978-1-78904-179-8

Digesting Recipes
The Art of Culinary Notation
Susannah Worth
A recipe is an instruction, the imperative tone of the expert,
but this constraint can offer its own kind of potential. A recipe
need not be a domestic trap but might instead offer escape –
something to fantasise about or aspire to.
Paperback: 978-1-78279-860-6 ebook: 978-1-78279-859-0

Most titles are published in paperback and as an ebook.
Paperbacks are available in traditional bookshops. Both print
and ebook formats are available online.
Follow us at:
https://www.facebook.com/ZeroBooks
https://twitter.com/Zer0Books
https://www.instagram.com/zero.Books